NARROW BOATING — FOR — BEGINNERS

What Americans need to know when considering a narrowboat vacation in the UK

Jennifer Petkus

Mallard Travel
Denver, Colorado

Narrowboating for Beginners

Published by Mallard Travel,
an imprint of Mallard Press, Denver, Colorado

ISBN 13: 978-0692608258
ISBN 10: 0692608257

Dedicated to my husband, Jim Bates, my best friend Lee Thomas, and her brother, Jim Thomas, for helping create some of the happiest memories of my life.

In recognition also of the men and women who built the canals, worked on them, restored them and now travel on them.

Gas Street Basin in Birmingham is the heart of the canal network. Here the Worcester & Birmingham Canal meets the Birmingham Canal Navigations

Contents

About this book

Why a Narrowboat Trip?

Canal history

Choosing a canal

The narrowboat

Life on board

How to steer a narrowboat

Mooring

Locks, bridges and tunnels

Knots and ropes

Etiquette / waterway rules

Checklist

Resources

Conclusion

Glossary

About this book

In many ways *Narrowboating for Beginners* is a book that doesn't really need to exist. After all, my husband and I and our friends took our first narrowboat trip without the benefit of such a book and lived to tell the tale. In fact most beginners show up for their first narrowboat trip without any idea what to expect.

Of course I had done some homework beforehand. I'd visited numerous canal-related websites, watched several YouTube videos about the canals and narrowboats, downloaded brochures from many boat hires, and read LTC Rolt's *Narrow Boat* and the *Boaters Handbook*, but none of that helped when I took the tiller that first day.

I was frankly terrified. I did get us out of the marina but I was so upset by the experience that I happily gave up the tiller to my husband and didn't drive the boat for another two days.

After that humiliation, I decided that perhaps I'd be better at turning locks, but even though I consider myself mechanically inclined, I was often doing stupid things like trying to open lock gates before the lock chamber had filled or trying to fill the chamber with a downhill paddle still open.

By the fourth or fifth lock, however, it started making sense and even steering the boat got easier, after my husband's suggestion of pointing the tiller at the thing you don't want to hit.

After a time, we were all decent at steering and turning a lock, but turning the boat around was still an all hands on deck emergency and reversing the boat was impossible. And many times we realized something very important only after it was too late to do any good. For instance, we found that our boat hire had kindly provided a *Pearson's Canal Companion* for us and if we'd only read it, we would have known there was a water point, a winding hole or a very good pub around the next bend. Another example was our last mooring when someone showed us the canalman's hitch, which would have saved us from all the times we'd tied our lines into Gordian knots.

So even though narrowboating isn't rocket science, there are still some little tricks and advice that I can offer by way of this book that should improve your first time on a narrowboat. Some things are pretty important, like keeping clear of the cill, some are trivial, like bring your own washcloth, and some will just make you say, "Oh, well that explains it," like the fact it's called a balance beam because it counterbalances the weight of the gate.

This book is primarily intended for Americans contemplating their first narrowboat vacation, but that doesn't mean someone in the UK won't find it useful (a UK edition where color is spelled *colour* may be forthcoming). Americans contemplating a canal trip assume that everyone in the UK has traveled a canal but on our trips, we kept encountering Britons who confessed it was their first trip. There are even people who live alongside a canal who have never been on a boat.

This book is not intended for people contemplating living aboard a narrowboat because there are already many good books on that subject. And this book doesn't

About these symbols

This is a tip icon, indicating some little idea that will make your narrowboat trip more enjoyable, like remembering to pack a flashlight for your walk back to the boat after a nice meal and drinks at a pub.

This is a note icon, indicating some information that's interesting, like the fact that LTC Rolt and Robert Aickman established the Inland Waterways Association in 1946.

This is a caution icon, indicating advice like don't drive your boat so fast that it leaves a wake, don't wear Crocs on a slippery boat and don't back up while standing next to the edge of the lock pound.

This is the danger icon, with advice like don't let your kids run along the top of a boat while it's in a lock, something I've actually seen.

This is the relax icon, reminding you that you really should enjoy your trip rather than try to go as many miles in a day as you can.

address pleasure boats, canoes, kayak or barges—just narrowboats. It is also intended for people traveling on canals and not navigable rivers. While much remains the same, there are special considerations when taking a narrowboat onto tidal or fast-moving waters.

This book is also not intended for people who plan to take out a narrowboat alone, although much of the information will still be pertinent. It's challenging to single-handedly turn a lock or moor, but it can be done.

Most people are glad of a little help, but solo boatees can be prickly. They take pride in their boating skills and some may prefer to do it on their own. Always ask before lending a hand.

Much of the information in this book can be found at my website, **NarrowboatingForBeginners.com**. Throughout the print edition of this book, you'll see QR codes and shortened URLs that link to online material. (Zeros are shown as 0.) Download an app for your smartphone or tablet to scan QR codes (available for **iOS** and **Android**) or enter the shortened URL.

This book is also available for the Kindle (or any computer, smartphone or tablet with the **Kindle App**). If you buy the paperback from Amazon, you will also receive the Kindle edition for free. If you buy the paperback at a bookstore, follow the instructions at the back of this book to receive a free copy for your Kindle reader or app.

Also, when a new print edition of this book is published, the Kindle version will be updated for free, so you need never be out of date.

Finally, this book is not meant as an alternative to reading *The Boater's Handbook* published by the Canal & River Trust (or the guides published by another appropriate waterway authority). Much of that information is repeated here, but consider the handbook to be definitive.

Narrowboating
ForBeginners.com
goo.gl/C2n3GS

Kindle
App
goo.gl/Aue8ED

QuickScan
for iOS
goo.gl/oMDEC5

Kindle
Edition
goo.gl/9UXSc6

QR Code Reader
for Android
goo.gl/tzGsg8

Why a Narrowboat Trip?

If you're reading this book, you're probably already planning to take a narrowboat vacation, but you may have friends who ask: what's the appeal of the canals? Of course the majority of your friends have no idea what a narrowboat is, about the history of the canals or the part they played in the Industrial Revolution. I'll address all that later, but first I thought I'd relate the various threads that drew me to narrowboating.

For some reason, I've always been fascinated by the thought of rivers and boats. When I was growing up in San Antonio, *Captain Gus* was the afternoon kids' show on the CBS affiliate television station KENS. More than once, I recall, the show played a serialized version of *Journey to the Beginning of Time*, which depicts four boys who visit the American Museum of Natural History in New York. The boys somehow take a rowboat down a river of time and view extinct animals like woolly mammoths and dinosaurs. The movie was shown in six-minute segments and I enjoyed it immensely. I'm sure it's responsible for many paleontology degrees.

Journey to the Beginning of Time was originally a 1955 Czech movie, *Cesta Do Praveku.* An American company filmed new opening and closing sequences and dubbed the dialog for serialization in the US. You can find some snippets on YouTube. VHS and DVD issues of the original Czech film are available. The 1975 *Three Men in a Boat* can also be found on YouTube, and it even inspired a BBC documentary by the same name.

Then just as I started college, I watched a BBC television adaptation of Jerome K. Jerome's book Three Men in a Boat W, about three Victorian men who take a skiff from Kingston upon Thames (now a suburb of London) to Oxford. It's a silly movie and a rambling book, following their misadventures that include being lost in the Hampton Court maze, trying to open a can of pineapple without a tin opener and the unpopularity of a banjo poorly played.

Three Men in a Boat, *Journey to the Beginning of Time*, *Huck Finn* and *The Heart of Darkness* somehow combined over the years into a desire to take a boat along the Thames or punt the Cam. It was further fueled by a 2001 trip to London when my husband and I walked along Regent's Canal, and the fire would be stoked again by reading *The Wench is Dead,* in Colin Dexter's Inspector Morse series, wherein Morse solves the death of a woman whose body was found in the Oxford Canal in 1859.

Unfortunately we weren't able to return to England until 2011 when we took our first narrowboat vacation. I was overjoyed to find that expectations matched reality but I also discovered that my childish enthusiasm had mellowed into a quiet enjoyment.

A narrowboat vacation is so unlike anything most Americans have experienced, especially for those of us from the larger states. We're accustomed to traveling cross-country, across time zones and through several states on interstate highways at 75 mph (or faster).

We plan trips where we visit both the Grand Canyon, Yellowstone and Glacier national parks in a car, station wagon, van, sport utility vehicle or motor home. Distance is the goal.

It's therefore hard to contemplate a trip at 2–3 mph where a full day of travel might only be 15 miles, and more likely 10 because you spent all day in a pub. Admittedly you might have spent several hours on a train or in a car getting to your boat hire, but once you're on the boat, you experience canal time and distance. You'll often have no television signal, no Internet access and sometimes no cellular access. You wake up with the sun and you go to sleep when it's dark.

It is important to relax on a narrowboat trip. Use it as an opportunity to display a side of your personality that you never get to use.

And yet a narrowboat trip isn't necessarily relaxing. As a beginner, you'll be pretty scared when you're handed the keys of a 60-foot-long, 15-ton metal boat after 30 minutes of instruction. You'll feel overwhelmed at your first lock, not really understanding how the darn thing works much less know what's the first thing to do. But these fears and worries are nothing like the fear of picking the wrong health plan, religious extremism or whether your 401K will survive.

You also might not relax because everything you see is new. You'll marvel at the genius of the Industrial Revolution and how two simple, wooden gates, a rack and pinion, sluices and paddles can lift a boat uphill or lower it downhill. You'll wonder: Is that bird a duck or a coot, a goose or a swan, a cormorant or a heron? You'll enjoy peeking into back gardens and looking at for sale signs and wishing you lived on the water. You'll slink away after a feral boat person *(See "Feral boat people" on page 64)* yells at you for leaving a wake. You'll curse or laugh at some hapless boat handler who rams your boat and then you'll remember that when you do the same later on.

I remember the line from Charles Dickens *A Christmas Carol* when Scrooge, after his conversion, "found that everything could yield him pleasure." Even standing in the rain while tying up the boat for the night is now a pleasant memory and afterward sitting with friends at the dinette table, sipping wine and eating cheese, will be one of the memories I cherish the rest of my life.

If you can find the right mix of people for your crew, it's an amazing opportunity to both test and deepen friendships. If you have children, it's a chance to spend time away from distractions. Parents and children alike are sobered looking down a deep lock as water comes gushing in to lift a boat. Opening and closing a lock gate has a primal satisfaction for young and old.

For weeks after your trip, you'll dream about the canal and suddenly realize how you should have negotiated that bridge. Every once in a while, in the shower, you'll feel your body sway to the slow dance of the boat.

I'm not alone in quoting from Kenneth Grahame's *The Wind in the Willows* Ⓦ when Ratty says to Mole: "Believe me, my young friend, there is nothing—absolutely nothing—half so much worth doing as simply messing about in boats."

The European water vole ("Ratty" in The Wind in the Willows) has all but disappeared from the canals. The CRT has conservation programs to encourage their return. Ⓦ

Other reasons you may enjoy narrowboating

Because you love history

If you're traveling the Bridgewater Canal, then you're really traveling history, for it was the first "true" canal in England, connecting the River Mersey and Liverpool with Manchester. It opened in 1761 (but not completed until 1776) because the 3rd Duke of Bridgewater needed to get his coal from Worsley to Manchester.

The Bridgewater Canal is not actually part of the Canal & River Trust, which manages most of the waterways in England and Wales. In fact there are several canals and navigations that remain separate from the CRT. It's easy to overlook some of these "hidden" canals.

If you visit the boat yard at Ellesmere, which is operated by the Canal & River Trust, you can see and hold some of the patterns used to cast parts for the Pontcysyllte Aqueduct, completed in 1805. When you visit the Harecastle Tunnel on the Trent and Mersey Canal, you can marvel at the fact there is no towpath. Boatmen would lie on their backs and "leg it" (using their legs to propel the boat) through the tunnel.

Actually there are two Harecastle tunnels. The first, engineered by James Brindley (who also consulted on the Bridgewater Canal), was completed in 1777 (when Brindley was five years dead). Brindley decided not to include a towpath through the tunnel because of the extra labor and engineering involved. Thomas Telford, the engineer who built the Pontcysyllte Aqueduct, built the second Harecastle tunnel in 1827 to relieve the congestion caused by the first tunnel (it took three hours to leg it), and aided by 50 years of engineering advancements, he added a towpath.

The Anderton Boat Lift, which was completed in 1875, connects the River Weaver and the Trent & Mersey Canal by lifting boats 50 feet, eliminating the need for a great number of locks.

Your narrowboat TARDIS makes further stops when you see the stonework of a bridge dated 1810 and the wooden gates of a lock dated 1999 (they last about 20 years). Or you travel right to the present when you visit the Falkirk Wheel Ⓦ, which opened in 2002 and looks like a piece of modern sculpture.

Because it's relatively affordable

A narrowboat vacation is affordable if you consider that you're paying for lodging, transportation and meals in one package, and if you're traveling with friends, you split the cost several ways. If you restrict yourself to enjoying the scenery, walking or cycling beside the boat and cooking all your meals on board, you'll save money, eat properly and get some exercise.

Or at least you can tell yourself that. Realistically you'll be tempted to visit pubs and local attractions such as steam railways and stately homes.

Because you like adventure, sort of

Another draw for me is the safe sort of adventure the canals offer. I'm still reasonably fit and active. I ride my bike, practice a martial art, hike and even climbed a 14,000-foot mountain recently (setting a world record for slowest ascent), but it's been years since my last whitewater rafting trip and my flirtation with rock climbing is a distant and painful memory. Nevertheless I still like a little adventure in my life and a narrowboat vacation is just about perfect.

Looking out over the edge of the boat while crossing an aqueduct is sufficient to get my heart pumping, passing through a tunnel cures me of any desire for spelunking and eating haggis or spotted dick is as far as I need to go to emulate Anthony Bourdain.

There's just enough real danger—falling into a lock or hanging up the boat on the cill—to keep you on your toes and just enough challenge—turning around in a winding hole or backing into a berth—to keep you from feeling complacent. If we ever do want to challenge ourselves, we can cruise in the off-off-months or take a boat out ourselves, without our friends. Two people are kept fairly busy turning a lock.

In fact a narrowboat vacation is just about perfect for an Anglophile middle-aged (OK, now senior) couple with an interest in history. But be warned. One trip is never enough.

An example of the history you might experience on a canal can be found at Worcester Cathedral, at one end of the Worcester & Birmingham Canal. The 11th-century cathedral is the grave of King John of Magna Carta infamy.

Navigating a narrowboat can be difficult and a boat's layout can be an important factor when choosing which boat to hire. The kitchen arrangement of this boat makes it pretty easy to pass through even when someone is cooking.

Three Men in a Boat
goo.gl/RCALRC

European Water Vole
goo.gl/Du38U7

The Wind in the Willows
goo.gl/VWUfaw

Bridgewater Canal
goo.gl/LuBpcb

Ellesmere boat yard
goo.gl/8qpZKp

Harecastle Tunnel
goo.gl/LErcYu

Anderton Boat Lift
goo.gl/WZyU5g

Falkirk Wheel
goo.gl/TFWeO0

You can still find narrowboats pulled by horses. Here Taff pulls an excursion boat near the source of the Llangollen Canal in Wales.

Canal history

Canals are a link to the past, a look to the future, either cutting edge or outdated almost the day a canal was completed. The canal system was fueled by the early days of the Industrial Revolution when the steam engine was an incredibly inefficient machine, useful only for pumping water out of coal mines.

The canal mania began in a time when wealthy landowners were consolidating their fields under the Enclosure Act, denying common grazing land rights that had been observed for centuries. Displaced farmworkers moved to the cities, further fueling the Industrial Revolution, which needed a way to get coal, potteries, lime, slate and timber to the cities and factories.

Canals were a response to the simple need to get raw materials to manufacturers and finished goods to market. They were a natural outgrowth of the use of rivers, then improvements to those rivers to make them into navigations and finally true canals.

They came into being when someone realized that on land a horse can pull a wheeled cart several times its weight, but it can pull a boat fifty times its weight over water. What's more, the horse can pull that weight for longer distances and at a constant speed—it didn't need to vary for delicate porcelain or raw iron ore.

The dizzying view from a boat crossing the Pontcysyllte Aqueduct in Wales.

Construction

For the most part the canals didn't require advanced technology. Instead most canals were dug by hand, using pick axes, shovels and wheelbarrows to dig and remove material. Gunpowder was occasionally used for blasting tunnels, but hand tools still did most of the work.

Clay was used to line the first "true" English canal, the Bridgewater, but there were skeptics who had argued the plan literally wouldn't hold water. James Brindley showed a Parliamentary committee it would work when he built a watertight trough with puddled clay in front of lawmakers in Whitehall. Restored canals are now lined with polyvinyl chloride and concrete, but puddled clay (clay mixed with water) tamped down by passing cattle worked for a century or more.

Many of the aqueduct and lock chambers were made of local stone, although apparently John Rennie regretted that when building the Avoncliff Aqueduct. The local stone cracked in the frost and has needed to be repaired several times. Rennie got it right, however, when he built the nearby Dundas Aqueduct.

Rennie had great success using cast iron, which was a relatively new structural material, having first been used in the 1770s for the Ironbridge that crosses the River Severn in Shropshire. Rennie used cast iron for several bridges, including the Southwark over the Thames in London.

Thomas Telford arguably created the most impressive cast-iron structure, the Pontcysyllte Aqueduct over the River Dee in Wales. The cast-iron trough is more than a thousand feet long and more than a hundred feet above the river valley. The trough rests on eighteen masonry piers held together with mortar that includes water, lime

One of the pillboxes along the Kennet & Avon Canal

The Falkirk Wheel in Scotland lifts boats 79 feet, connecting the Union and Forth & Clyde canals. It is the only boat lift of its kind in the world.

and oxblood. The cast iron trough is joined by strips of Welsh flannel dipped in boiling sugar and covered in molten lead. It remains today largely as Telford originally designed it.

Early canals slavishly followed natural contours, avoiding great spans, and as a consequence meandered.

As engineers gained knowledge they began to use locks to quickly gain and lose elevation. Soon they were conquering considerable changes in elevation via staircase locks, such as the Bingley Five-Rise Locks Ⓦ on the Leeds & Liverpool Canal, which climbs 59 feet over a distance of 320 feet.

America also has a rich history of canals, but as in Britain the canals declined as railroads expanded. Nevertheless, you can still travel US canals, including the Erie and the Chesapeake & Ohio canals.

Although canals were a considerable gamble, rarely being completed in time and always over budget, they could return substantial profits once completed and could cut transit times from weeks to days. Canal mania set in during the 1790s, especially as England was at war with France. Being able to move goods around England and Wales without braving French warships and the weather of the English Channel was a considerable incentive. (It's interesting that Britain caught the canal mania from the French.)

Soon various canal companies were crisscrossing the country, joining London to Bristol, Bristol to Birmingham, Liverpool to Manchester and Liverpool to Leeds. There was no coordination to these schemes, except possibly through the process of obtaining a royal assent to build a canal. Almost every canal was built by private enterprise but somehow the haphazard process resulted in a waterway infrastructure that fostered the Industrial Revolution. Soon every sort of manufacturer had easy access to a canal. In Wales, slate miners and lime producers could use the Llangollen branch to connect to the Shropshire Union Canal and from there to the rest of England. Cadbury Chocolate even built a model factory town alongside the Worcester & Birmingham Canal at Bournville. Josiah Wedgwood built his Etruria pottery business alongside the Trent & Mersey Canal, taking advantage of the narrowboat's gentle ride to ensure his wares reached their destination undamaged.

Competition and decline

The steam engine has a strange relationship with the canals. Coal carried on narrowboats fueled those early engines and as the engines became more sophisticated, their use expanded and the demand for coal increased.

Some of these early steam engines were used to pump water from rivers to feed aqueducts, like the steam engine at the Crofton pumping station on the Kennet and Avon, which began working in 1809 while Jane Austen was still alive.

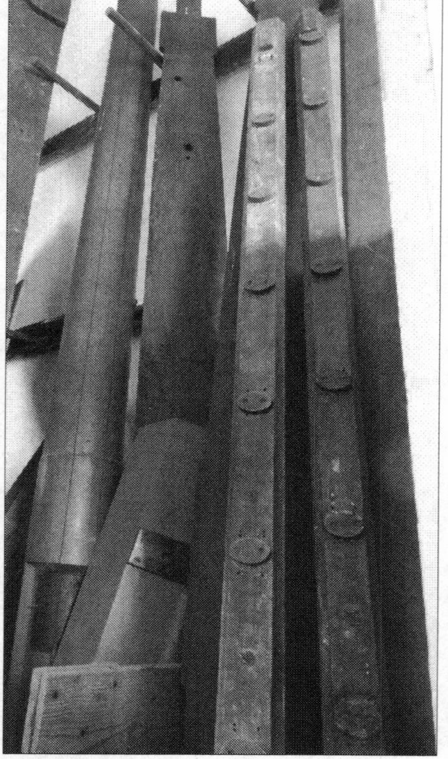

Railing pattern at the Ellesmere boat yard. These may be the model for the Pontcysyllte Aqueduct railings, still useful 200 years later.

By 1825, however, the Stockton & Darlington Railway was using steam locomotives to haul coal and soon the rapidly expanding railways saw the canals as competition. So companies like the Great Western Railway actually bought canals like the Kennet & Avon, increasing tolls on the K&A to make it less competitive and instituted the 4 mph speed limit narrowboaters still observe today.

In some cases the railways were required to maintain the canals they owned because of the royal assents that had created those canals, but in actual practice the canals would be neglected to the point of becoming unusable. Occasionally, however, a railway had a vested interest in maintaining a canal if that canal competed against a rival railway.

Some canal companies responded to competition by slashing their tolls while others tried to reinvent as railway companies. Cruelly the canals had transported a lot of the coal and timber that had helped build the railways and the same navvies (called that because they first worked on navigations—rivers improved to make them navigable) who had built the canals now worked on the railways. And as canal companies collapsed, canal beds would be turned into railroad beds.

The Great Western Railway wanted to stop the fly-boats and swift-boats on the K&A, which carried passengers at the breakneck speed of 10 mph. Most boats had obeyed the 4 mph speed limit (a brisk walking pace) to prevent leaving a wake that could erode canal banks. But swift-boats pulled by horses traveled on a standing wave that traveled with the boats, leaving little wake and offering little resistance.

Nevertheless the canal system survived into the twentieth century. During World War II, transportation by canal was still so important that when boatmen were called to service, women volunteers were taught to operate narrowboats for the Inland Waterways Department. Because of the initials "IW" on their work clothes, the older boatmen still working called them "idle women."

The Royal Military Canal along the Kent coast predates the GHQ line. It was created to foil another would-be invader—Napoleon Bonaparte. Although never intended to carry boat traffic, barges operated on the Royal Military Canal W until 1909.

Even the canals that had fallen out of use were still important to the war effort as they were a ready made barrier to a feared German invasion. Pillboxes and tank traps were built alongside canals and you can still see them on the Kennet & Avon, the Basingstoke, the Leeds & Liverpool, the Stroudwater, the Bridgewater & Taunton and other canals. They were part of the GHQ line and would have been defended by the Home Guard—"Dad's Army."

Time, however, was not on the side of the canals. After the railroads taking business from the canals came the motorways. The death knell was the Great Freeze of 1962-1963 when the canals iced over. Boats were stuck with the goods they carried for weeks. Any remaining business went to road and rail transport. The canals were left to disintegrate.

Recovery

But even while the canals were declining, there were individuals who recognized what would be lost by the death of the canals. At the start of World War II, Lionel Thomas Caswall (LTC or Tom) Rolt and his wife Angela had decided to live on board a narrowboat they had turned into a home. His account of their life aboard the Cressy, *Narrow Boat*, became an unlikely best seller. Their four-month voyage on the Oxford, Grand Union and Trent & Mersey canals inspired another author, Robert Aickman, to contact Rolt and together the men became the nucleus of the Inland Waterways Association, which in 1946 became a charitable trust that would promote, conserve and restore the canals.

Of course it took some time for that to happen. When the railways were nationalized (put under government control) in 1948, the canals they owned were transferred to the British Transport Commission. In 1962 the canals became part of the British Waterways Board and later British Waterways, a quasi-autonomous non-governmental agency or quango. Then in 2012, the Canal & River Trust was created as a charitable trust. CRT took over the assets of British Waterways, except for the Scottish canals, which remain under the control of the Scottish government.

Today the canals no longer carry goods but are instead tourist attractions. The Falkirk Wheel, which joins two Scottish canals, transports more tourists on its tour boats than cross it in narrowboats. What was once an Industrial Revolution superhighway is now a sedate and unhurried way to relax. Canals mix history, because you

Many narrowboats are decorated with canal art featuring roses and castles. No one's quite sure how, when or where the custom originated, but the first written record is from the mid-nineteenth century. You'll see the artwork on doors, water cans and barrels. A castle painting should have the following: a castle, bridge, water, swans (on the water and flying), trees, sailboats, clouds and mountains.

can find horse-drawn boats next to restored steam trains next to high-speed rail. You'll see canal side development, like grocery stores and factories converted into fashionable apartments, but you'll also find stretches of farmland and forest and you can still eat blackberries along the towpath. Canals combine the old and the new and somehow make it timeless.

Where you find canals, you can probably find a nearby heritage railway. The Llangollen Railway is a volunteer-run line from Llangollen to Corwen.

Avoncliff Aqueduct
goo.gl/0QcybF

Bingley Five-Rise Locks
goo.gl/foc7Ne

Dundas Aqueduct
goo.gl/ETlW4k

Crofton Beam Engine
goo.gl/lEYwCF

Pontcysyllte Aqueduct
goo.gl/zdG8EQ

Royal Military Canal
goo.gl/PvnOcc

Choosing a canal

Trying to pick your first canal is like trying to pick a favorite pet or child. Each one has its own delights, challenges and oddities despite overall similarities like quaint pubs, beautiful scenery and astounding engineering. In choosing, you have to balance your abilities versus your desires, your craving for solitude versus the canal's popularity and your itinerary versus the canal's accessibility.

How to choose

We plan our infrequent UK vacations around our canal trips, but our choice of canal is also influenced by those cities or attractions we wish to visit.

If you're interested in the Industrial Revolution and impressed by Georgian engineering, then consider the Birmingham Canal Navigations Ⓦ. After all, Matthew Boulton chose to build his Soho Foundry beside the canal. With his partner James Watt, Boulton sold hundreds of steam engines for use in mines and factories. And the canal boasts the Tardebigge Flight of 30 locks

Shakespeare's birthplace in Stratford-Upon-Avon is just a short distance from the canal.

stretching two-and-a-quarter miles, the longest flight of locks in the UK.

If you're fond of William Shakespeare, you might visit Stratford-upon-Avon Ⓦ and travel the similarly named canal. The canal connects with the River Avon just a short walk (less than 10 minutes) from the Bard's birthplace. The 25-mile canal extends all the way to Birmingham (if you include the Worcester & Birmingham Canal).

If you're a Janeite, the obvious city to visit is Bath in Somerset. Jane Austen lived here from 1801 to 1805, just as the Kennet & Avon Canal Ⓦ was being built. From Bath, a UNESCO World Heritage Site, you go east on the canal toward Devizes and the stunning Caen Hill flight of 16 locks, one of the Seven Wonders of the Waterways. From Devizes, you can easily visit Stonehenge, another World Heritage Site.

If you prefer the Brontës, then the brooding Pennines and the Rochdale Canal Ⓦ might be your choice. You can even hire your narrowboat from Bronte Boats. The Brontë parsonage in Haworth is about a 30-minute drive from the canal.

If mystery is your thing, then the dreaming spires of Oxford might appeal, especially if you're a fan of Inspector Morse. If you've watched the ITV television series of *Inspector Morse*, *Lewis* or *Endeavour*, then you frequently saw the Oxford Canal Ⓦ and any number of narrowboats. From Oxford, you can join the Grand Union Canal network that can take you to Leicester and Birmingham or even back to Stratford.

The Grand Union also goes to London, of course. If you're determined to visit the city that Sherlock Holmes' friend and biographer Doctor Watson described as "that great cesspool into which all the loungers and idlers of the Empire are irresistibly drained," then you can travel the very urban Regent's Canal Ⓦ, but be prepared for drunken revelers, graffiti and *très chic* boatees wearing Wayfarers and fashionably louche nautical wear.

Regent's Canal, alas, has become fashionable, but it's

Caen Hill flight of 16 locks. An expert crew might manage this in four hours.

still an amazing mixture of gritty urbanism, like the very touristy Camden Locks, and the picturesque, like Little Venice in Maida Vale. It also has its serene moments when your narrowboat putts through Regent's Park and the backside of London Zoo.

Practicalities

So first pick your canal based on some connection you have to a city, a region, an author or even your favorite football club. Then start to consider the practicalities.

Although they're called mid-week breaks, implying Monday through Friday, most boat hires have some flexibility. The same isn't true for weekend breaks, which start on Friday.

Days vs distance

How many days your first canal trip should be obviously depends on the type of person you are. If you want to tour ruined castles or make brass rubbings at parish churches or enjoy a village concert, then you're not going to get very far and may have to plan a longer trip. On our boat trips, we've explored said ruined castles, visited narrowboat museums, marveled at lock flights, lingered over pub lunches and even rented taxis to explore the countryside. Your crew, however, may be content to rack up the miles, eating most of your meals onboard and avoid brass rubbings and drafty castles.

Senior (often called concession) discounts in the UK may start at age 60. Although boat hires rarely offer a senior discount (they'd go out of business), most attractions like museums, castles and stately homes do.

For your first trip, I recommend a mid-week break, which is four nights and five days, returning the boat on the fifth day. So how far can you get in that amount of time, considering that you're traveling between 2 and 3 mph? It all depends on the number of locks and swing bridges, but using the worksheet above, about 43 miles is realistic, assuming 10 locks and three swing bridges. Then start estimating how many stately homes and museums you want to visit to see whether you can get it done in the remaining hours.

A mid-week break is just long enough to be relaxing and will leave you wanting to come back. If you're traveling with friends, five days together shouldn't have strained the friendship and will give you an idea whether you want to travel together on another boat trip.

Ring cycle

For the same reason, I recommend against planning a ring route for your first trip. The advantage of a ring is that instead of retracing your journey to return your boat, you can make a loop by traveling more than one canal. The Four Counties Ring (W), for instance, including the Shropshire Union, the Staffordshire & Worcestershire, and the Trent & Mersey canals, can be done in a week if you travel eight hours a day, but that's a lot of pressure for a beginner crew.

How much does it cost?

Renting a narrowboat is surprisingly affordable, depending on the exchange rate and time of year, of course. For instance, I just checked the price of a boat that sleeps up to six to pick up in Bath on the Kennet & Avon Canal for a mid-week break in September (pick up the boat that Monday afternoon and return it Friday morning).

Cost of the boat for four nights, five days: £1,100
Fuel deposit: £50 (you're credited for unused fuel)
Damage deposit: £50
Cancellation insurance: £25
Subtotal: £1,225 (at 02/2018 conversion rate—$1,700)
Divided by four nights: $425
Per person/per night (crew of four): $106

How far can you travel during a mid-week break?

Number of hours
Day 1: 3 hours (pick up boat at 3 p.m.)
Day 2: 7 hours
Day 3: 6 hours
Day 4: 9 hours
Day 5: 1 hour (return by 9 a.m.)
Total: 26 hours

Minus lock time
Number of locks: 10 locks x 2 = 20
Number of swing bridges: 3 bridge x 2 = 6
@ 20 minutes per lock/bridge: 8.7 hours
Net hours: 17.3 hours

Total distance traveled
17.3 hours @ 2.5 mph = 43.25 miles

Number of locks

You might want to choose a canal with relatively few locks or at least consider what route avoids the highest concentration of locks. I'd recommend a beginner not attempt Caen Hill, for instance, but you can avoid it if you confine your canal journey to the Bath to Devizes portion of the canal, stopping (or beginning) at Foxhanger Wharf in Devizes.

Some authorities suggest beginners choose a lock-free canal, like the 42 restored miles of the Lancaster Canal W that almost makes it to the Lake District, but locks are an essential part of the experience, I think.

Wide vs narrow canal

I recommend a beginner pick a wide canal with locks that can accommodate two narrowboats abreast (at least 14 feet wide), because that means your narrowboat will easily navigate through the many bridges and locks you'll encounter. The downside is that larger locks take longer to fill and drain and you'll often share locks with other boats, but that just gives you more time to chat with other boaters.

Popularity

Popular canals also mean more traffic. I'm not suggesting you intentionally pick an unpopular canal—just be aware that your expectation of how much distance you travel each day may be unrealistic, especially during summer. An advantage of a popular canal, however, is that you'll be able to fully research the canal before you arrive. You'll find more books and documentaries about the Llangollen and Kennet & Avon canals than the isolated Monmouthshire & Brecon Canal Ⓦ in Wales, picturesque though it is.

Transportation, laundry, groceries, towpath, pubs

Other practicalities include transportation to your canal.

Various ways to save on a boat hire

- Book early, before the end of the year for a trip in the following year
- Pay cash, sending a bank transfer rather than credit card
- Although rare, the boat hire may offer concessions (discounts) for seniors and children
- Book a flotilla, if you can convince enough people to join you that you require two or more boats!
- Ask about canceled or one-way trips. Last-minute cancellations do happen and occasionally boat hires need someone to move boats to another base and you get to save on a one-way trip.
- Book yearly, some boat hires have increasing discounts each year you travel. Loyalty rewards, however, usually require no more than a 12-month gap between bookings, but it never hurts to ask.

Sadly you usually can't combine multiple discounts

Are you brave enough to drive on the left side of the road and negotiate roundabouts? Or do you prefer to take the train? Are there grocery stores on your route? If you're going for distance, you'll need to cook and eat your meals on board. Are there laundries in the towns and villages along your route?

And even though you take a narrowboat trip to get away from it all, most of us can't ignore work and family completely. Frequently we've had little or no cell service on our trips, so you might want to choose a canal that goes through moderately large towns if you need to stay connected.

All canals have towpaths, although the quality of the path varies widely. One of the great delights of a canal trip is walking along beside your boat, so look up the quality of the towpath. Some towpaths are challenging on a bike, something to consider if you rent a bike.

Pubs are very common, but check your route and your timings. We've moored up in the middle of nowhere with not a pub in sight, meaning another night without a hot meal and a local ale.

Time of year

The time of year will also affect your trip. We always travel in the spring or fall, during the off season. The canals are less congested and we've had decent weather, even in Wales. Just be aware if you plan too late or too early, some of the attractions you hope to visit may not be open. Savings can be significant depending on the season. Early September is a great time to book a trip. There are still many fall festivals but the kids are back in school, meaning fewer boats on the canals.

Picking a boat hire

Your experience on the canal will also depend on the boat hire you use. The search term "narrowboat hire" should return pages and pages of results. Some of those results are to specific boat hires and some to booking services, the clue will be if they let you inquire about any waterway or canal in the whole of the UK. Booking services may have an additional fee and some boat hires will say it's cheaper to book directly with them.

If possible, choose a boat hire that's convenient to a lock so that you can get hands-on training turning a lock.

Some of the boat hires have bases on several canals; some are specific to a canal or ring. You may want to use a larger boat hire with bases on many canals if you hope to use a yearly loyalty reward and travel different canals. On isolated waterways, you may not find many boat hire companies. You can also look for boat owners who hire out their boats in the canal newspapers and magazines listed in the Resources chapter.

Search for reviews of the boat hire you want to use. Just be aware that online reviews should be taken with a grain of salt.

Direction

The boat hire you choose may determine which direction you travel on the canal. If the boatyard is at one end of the canal, you'll probably travel out in the opposite direction. And it's a silly thing, but if you have a guidebook to your canal, look in which direction the guide is oriented. If the pages read east to west, it's a lot more convenient to travel east to west. Of course it will still be backward on the return trip, but by then you won't need the guide as much.

Return

You will almost always have to return the boat from where you picked it up. You generally pick up the boat in the afternoon and return it early in the morning.

Cancellation fee/insurance

Most boat hires offer a cancellation fee that will protect you should you or a member of the crew become ill or if there's a death in the family. The cancellation fee is prob-

Two hotel boats share a lock. If you want to ease yourself into narrowboating, you can always book a cruise on a hotel boat, where you get to enjoy the canal without needing to drive or turn a lock and a chef prepares your meals.

ably about £50 for a week-long trip and I recommend paying it. You can waive this if you have trip insurance, but you'll have to supply proof of this. (Trip insurance still might not cover a narrowboat rental.) Some credit card companies offer trip cancellation insurance for travel booked on common carriers, such as airline and train travel, but again it probably doesn't cover hiring a narrowboat. Also, you would have to have paid for the trip with that credit card.

You really can't go wrong

Every time we watch a documentary about a specific canal, that's the canal we want to travel next. It seems every canal has something to offer, so I doubt you can really go wrong just picking one at random, but once you've picked one, I suggest you study it thoroughly. A 30-lock flight is something for which you want to be prepared.

Birmingham Canal Navigations
goo.gl/7PsdZM

Stratford-upon-Avon Canal
goo.gl/RcKkQh

Kennet & Avon Canal
goo.gl/L8j22R

Rochdale Canal
goo.gl/xjOmGT

Oxford Canal
goo.gl/cgr4gv

Regent's Canal
goo.gl/sL0JW8

Four Counties Ring
goo.gl/voyz9r

Lancaster Canal
goo.gl/1C9sp5

Monmouthshire & Brecon Canal
goo.gl/68EYgN

The River Avon flows just by Holy Trinity Church where Shakespeare is buried. Narrowboats can navigate the river or the nearby Stratford-upon-Avon Canal.

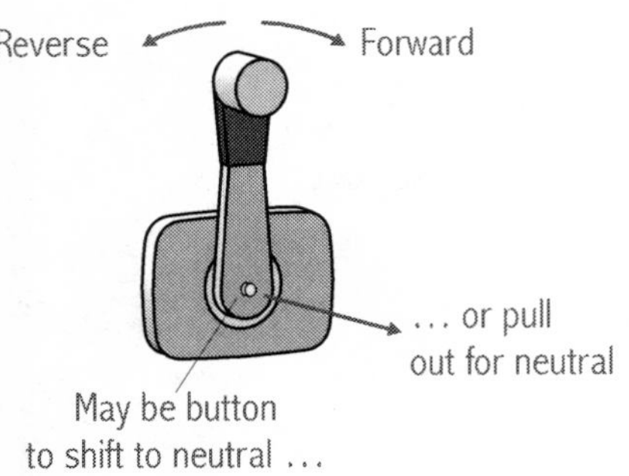

The throttle or speed lever is very simple: push forward to go forward and pull back for reverse, the farther you push or pull the faster you go forward or back. On some throttle levers, you press a button to shift to neutral. On others, you pull the throttle away from the box to shift to neutral.

The narrowboat

Narrowboats live up to their name. They're less than seven feet wide and a boat that can comfortably accommodate four passengers is about 60 feet long. They're steered from the rear by a person standing in the open turning a tiller. Some private boats are equipped with a steering wheel and a covered stern, but you're unlikely to hire such a boat.

Starting up

Narrowboats are powered by a diesel engine in the rear of the boat. The engine goes "putt-putt-putt," but not

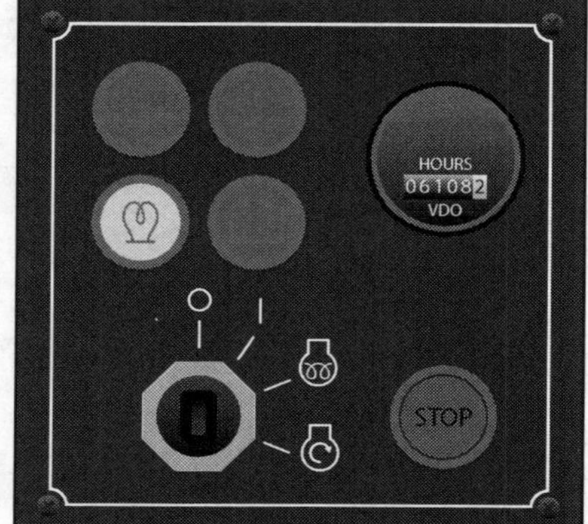

so loudly to be annoying and you won't even hear it from the front of the boat. Starting the engine is a simple procedure but there are a number of steps you have to follow.

1. First, put the throttle in neutral (by pressing a button or pulling the throttle out)
2. Insert the ignition key into the control panel.
   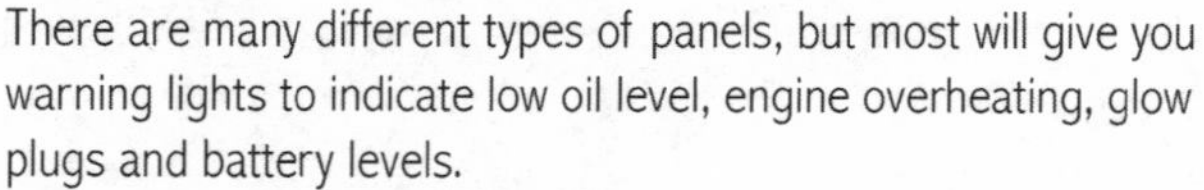
   There are many different types of panels, but most will give you warning lights to indicate low oil level, engine overheating, glow plugs and battery levels.
3. Turn the key to the ON position—you'll hear an obnoxious tone indicating you have battery power. Then turn the key to the GLOW plug position (looks like a light bulb in the picture above), which heats the glow plugs. Leave in this position only a few seconds before …

Diesel engines don't have spark plugs and instead rely on the heat of compression to ignite the fuel, but a cold engine is hard to start, thus the glow plugs to heat the fuel before turning over the engine.

4. … turning key to the START position (light bulb with a curved arrow) and holding until the engine catches.
5. Once started, you can release the key, which will return to the run position. Press STOP to stop the engine before switching the key to the off position.

Bilge pump

You may also be instructed to operate the bilge pump after starting the engine, but on many boats, it runs automatically.

Layout

The layout of most boats is similar. There's open seating in the front (the well deck) that's not very comfortable but you can't beat the view. The best seats face forward. Some seats (benches, actually) face backward, requiring you to turn around to see ahead.

ALWAYS PUSH the rear hatch completely open during the day. Even moderately tall people (5'8") can easily whack the top of the head on the edge of the hatch if it's not completely open. Stepping out through the double doors in the front of the boat is also tricky. And after tying up the stern line, make sure the tiller is not over you when you stand up. It took two nasty bruises before I learned to check for this.

If you're of unusual stature or girth, negotiating the interior of a narrowboat can be a challenge. A 6-foot-tall person can stand upright inside most boats but a narrowboat roof is bowed and the walls slope inward. Traveling the length of a narrowboat is also a challenge. The passage next to the main berth and bathroom is quite narrow and those sloping walls don't help. You quickly learn to walk like an Egyptian. Carefully study the floor plan, especially the kitchen layout, of a boat you're considering hiring if you have difficulty negotiating sharp turns. The location of the counter opposite the sink is very important and when possible, choose a boat where the sink, cooker and refrigerator are on the same side of the boat.

Carefully inspect larger boats before you leave the boat hire. These are difficult for the boat hire to clean in the turnaround time and partiers find ingenious places to leave behind unpleasant surprises.

Pricing

If you go online to book a boat, you'll need to specify the number of passengers, which canal, length of stay and the departure date. Boat hires sort their boat by number of passengers, number of toilets, amenities and stern styles. Those criteria go into assigning a boat to

Create a checklist of questions to ask and skills to learn when picking up your boat. You'll want to know how to:

- ☐ Steer the boat, turn around and reverse
- ☐ Turn a lock
- ☐ Moor the boat
- ☐ Turn on the cabin heater, switch propane tanks
- ☐ Turn on the bath/shower pump
- ☐ Perform daily maintenance checks
- ☐ Turn off/on the DC-to-AC inverter
- ☐ Find the fire extinguishers and fire blanket
- ☐ Find the first-aid kit and flashlight
- ☐ Sound the horn and light the headlamp
- ☐ Wear and use the life jacket

a pricing band. That price band is sort of a multiplier when calculating the cost of a boat on a certain day. You'll pay more for that boat in the summer, less in the fall and spring. Bank holidays also affect pricing.

The number of passengers is probably the biggest criteria in assigning a boat to a pricing band and it also determines the length of the boat. A 2-4 person boat comfortably fits two, a 4-6 person boat comfortably fits four, and so on. The upper passenger limit is about 12 and these are essentially party boats.

Larger boats generally have bunk beds or single beds on either side or both. A dinette table usually converts to a double bed. A narrowboat double bed is quite narrow and short, however the aisle side of the double bed in the center of the boat usually has nothing at the foot, so a larger person can stretch out without disturbing the bedding, made easier because of the lack of a top sheet *(See "Duvets" on page 53)*.

Realistically most boats are very similar and often amenities such as a second toilet, Wi-Fi (*de rigueur* in 2018), a microwave, extra closets or a fireplace can significantly affect how much you pay.

A Tale of Two Boats

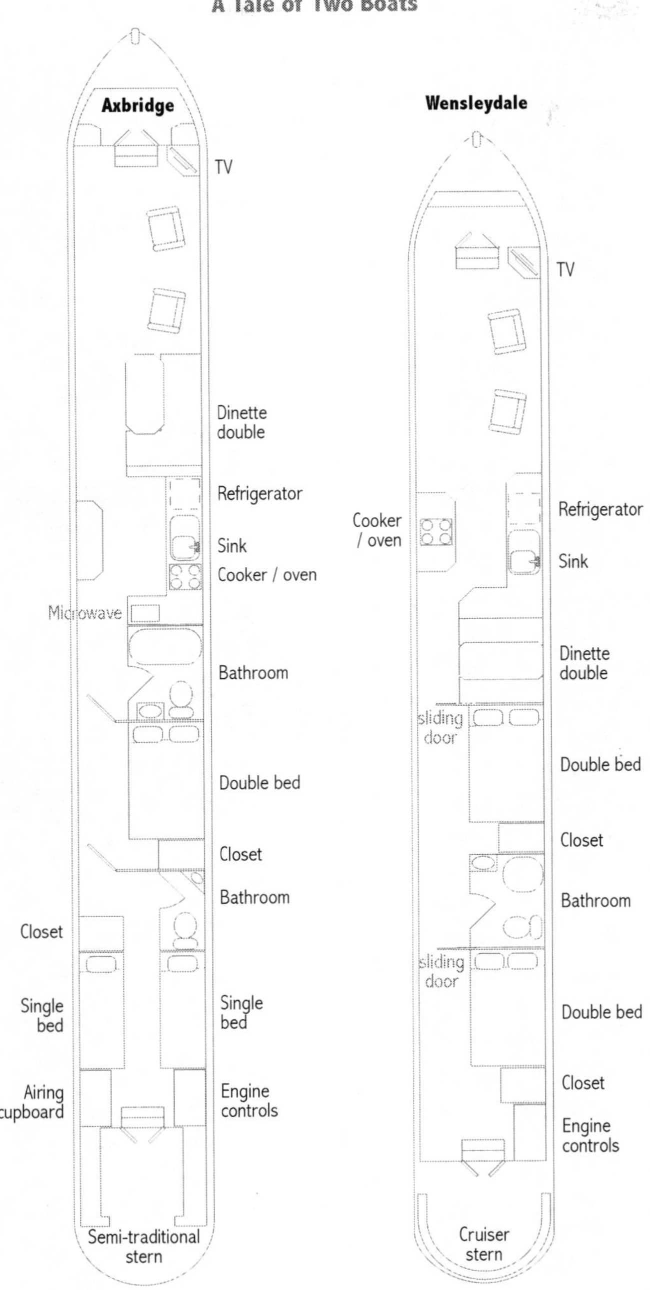

Single toilet

Traditional stern

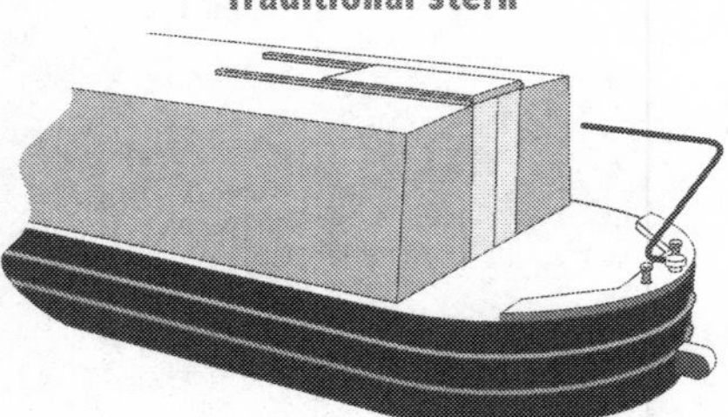

Semi-traditional stern

Cruiser stern

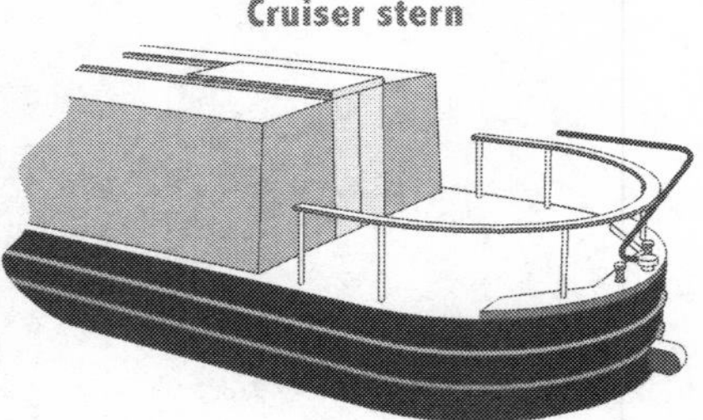

Four people can probably share a single toilet for a mid-week break (four nights, return early the fifth day) assuming no intestinal distress, but not an entire week (seven nights, return the eighth day).

In my experience, there's no problem with four people sharing a single toilet except at night. In the example boat layout on the previous page, you'll see that on the Axbridge, someone sleeping on the dinette double in the front of the boat can reach the main bathroom without passing by the people sleeping in the double bed in the middle of the boat. On the Wensleydale, however, the person sleeping on the dinette double must open a door to get to the bathroom, possibly awakening the sleepers in the double bed. And on the Wensleydale, the person sleeping on the double bed in the rear of the boat also has to open a door to get to the bathroom.

The Wensleydale, though still a very nice boat, has another disadvantage compared to the Axbridge. The kitchen arrangement makes it difficult for people to pass one another. You quickly learn to back up or sit at the dinette to let someone through. These are admittedly minor quibbles, but after a week on a boat with four people, the little things add up.

Of course the Wensleydale is a cheaper boat than the

Axbridge because it's shorter and has the single bathroom, but you may decide that in the long run you'd be better off with the more expensive boat, especially if you have to unexpectedly rush back to the marina to pump out that single toilet's storage tank.

A shorter boat, while it may be cramped or lack some luxuries, is a little more maneuverable, especially in a narrow canal. A very short boat, like a day boat, however, is a little *too* maneuverable.

You'll also be surprised how little things like the fact that the Wensleydale has sliding doors for the central bedroom gets very annoying. As the boat lists (tilts), the doors will unexpectedly slide open or shut because the latches that hold the door in place are easily dislodged. You can walk through a door, turn around because someone called your name and then walk right into a closed door when you turn around! The Axbridge also had many more little shelves to hold belongings, which becomes very important. So when looking at a price band, realize some of the little things are important.

Then again, how do you put a price on the fact that when other boaters pass the Wensleydale, they shout, "Cheese, Gromit!"

I prefer the cruiser stern because there's more room to stand in front of the tiller, making it easier to gauge clearances when passing through bridges and entering locks. Cruiser sterns have probably also saved a few people from falling off the end of the boat although that might be balanced against those people who've fallen off the railing and into the canal.

Stern styles

Your choices are traditional, semi-traditional or cruiser style, but few boat hires offer traditional, which provides only enough space for the person at the tiller to stand (it does, however, offer more cabin space). Semi-traditional has two benches on either side of the boat in front of the tiller, protected by side walls but open to the top. This allows several people to keep the boat driver company but takes away from cabin space and so is usually found on longer boats. The cruiser stern is larger with a half-moon railing to allow others to perch beside the driver. Several people can occupy a cruiser stern, but remember to leave space for full turns of the tillers.

Conveniences

Conveniences include microwaves, extra closets, shelves, Wi-Fi, multiple three-prong outlets, airing cupboards (where you can hang damp clothes), additional toilets, wood stoves, toaster, coffee maker. Some boat hires offer first-class boats that feature expensive wood paneling and granite counter tops. Such boats usually are longer.

Consider yourself fortunate if you hire a boat with Wi-Fi, but test the connectivity before you leave the boat hire. Ask for help if you can't connect but don't be surprised if the hire staff gives you a blank look. They're probably a lot more knowledgeable about turning a lock than upgrading your OS. Of course even if you can connect to the router, it only works if the boat is in cellular range and often speed and data are limited. The Wi-Fi is there to check your email, not binge watch Netflix.

Picking up the boat / returning

Most boat hires will have you pick up the boat in the afternoon, to give the cleaning staff time to prepare the boats returned that morning. You may pay a penalty if you're late to pick up or return a boat. By the way, remember to wash dishes and generally clean up after yourself before returning the boat if you don't want to eat the damage deposit.

Some canals are deeper than you think and locks can be very deep. You'll notice that Canal & River Trust employees and volunteers are always photographed wearing buoyancy aids.

Buoyancy aids / life jackets

You may have to ask the boat hire for them, but realistically few people ask. I strongly recommend them for children. Some canals are so shallow that someone who falls in could simply stand up to avoid drowning, but people do drown in the canals. Locks are especially dangerous with steep sides and deep water.

Terms and conditions

Drinking and driving

I think most boat hires are aware that people on the water will consume alcohol. Check your terms and conditions. Obviously you should not drive the boat when under the influence of alcohol.

Definitely don't drink or text or take selfies while turning a lock.

Child drivers / pets

Check your terms and conditions but usually children can drive a boat when under the supervision of an adult. Most boat hires allow pets but might require a damage deposit. You probably didn't bring a pet with you from the states, but if you have UK friends on your boat, make sure their dog won't cost you the deposit.

Repairs

If your boat does break down, immediately call your boat hire. Don't call a boatyard to have someone fix your boat, because you'll probably have to pay for those repairs out of your own pocket.

DANGER! Engine checks should be done with the engine turned off, especially when checking the propeller shaft for weeds. It's not good enough to put the throttle lever in neutral because it can slip back into gear. Oil and water levels should be checked on a cold engine (or at least turned off for about 15 minutes).

Driving hours

You can drive from sunrise to sunset. It shouldn't be so dark that you need to turn on the headlight.

Daily maintenance

Your boat hire will tell you what you need to do each day to keep your boat shipshape. It's unlikely that forgetting a daily check will cause a disaster, but driving without enough oil or water could damage the engine and probably make you liable for any repair costs.

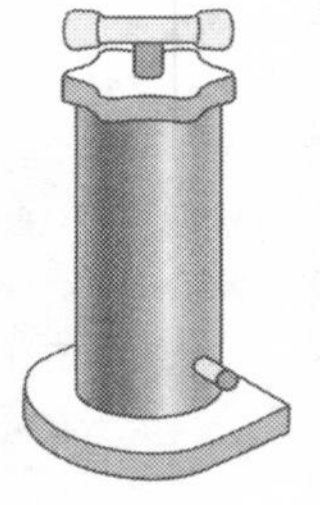

So it's best to check the oil dipstick and the radiator as directed. You'll probably also need to turn the stern gland greaser (looks like a miniature bicycle

pump, detonator or antique fire extinguisher) at the end of the day. It should be done after the engine has been running, although **turn off** the engine before removing the deck plates and climbing down into the engine well. All you need do is turn the greaser handle clockwise until you feel resistance. That's enough to force grease into the housing where the drive and propeller shafts meet.

It's unrealistic to expect that anyone will read the boat manual word-for-word, but it's a good idea to at least leaf through the manual and an even better idea if several people do so. Hopefully one of the crew will remember some important piece of information when needed.

The greaser is probably near the propeller shaft, although on some boats it's located more conveniently. Your boat hire will tell you where it is or you can find that information in the boat manual.

You should also check to make sure the propeller shaft isn't wrapped in weeds by looking through the weed hatch. It's an unpleasant task because you have to put your hand into the water and feel around the shaft. Of course the propeller shaft is never choked with weeds until it is, usually at a very inconvenient time.

Opening the weed hatch (with the engine off!) is easy but may take some jiggling. The screw presses down the lid against the weed hatch. Loosen by turning counter-clockwise and remove the bar by sliding it left or right and then angling it up. Once the bar is removed, you can remove the lid. Then reach down to inspect the propeller shaft.

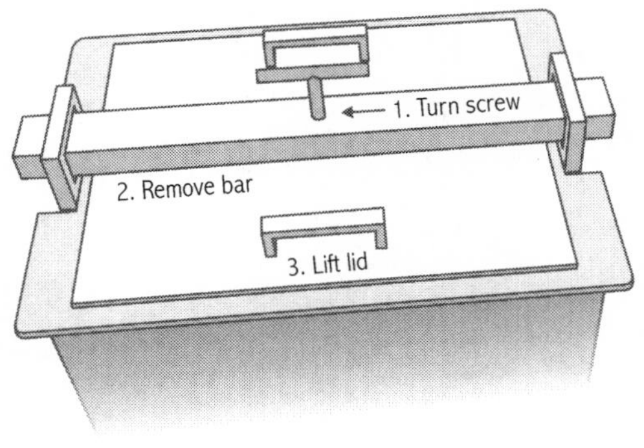

When replacing the lid, make sure the bar is centered within the two slots on either side of the hatch.

Forgetting to replace the weed hatch (or improperly securing it) can eventually sink the boat.

Fuel, water and waste

Unfortunately there are usually no gauges for any of the fluid levels on hire boats. As mentioned earlier, the boat hire will provide you with enough fuel for most trips, just tell them how far you plan to go. You might be able to refuel at another boat yard occupied by your boat hire and get a discount.

If some of these maintenance checks stress you, relax. They take perhaps 15–20 minutes a day and after they've been done a few times are automatic. It really is very easy to operate a narrowboat.

Take on water whenever possible for two reasons: one, filling the tank is a slow process if you let it go too long, and two, you don't want to run out of water just when you worked up a full head of shampoo lather.

Judging when you've filled up the waste tank is even more difficult. Your boat manual might mention that if you can see waste up to a certain line, you should stop using the toilet, by which time, of course, it's too late.

Life on board

A typical day

Last night you moored just when dusk was falling. You ate dinner at a pub, a 17th-century building you learned was in a scene from *The Remains of the Day*. In the next booth a pleasant obviously retired couple from Kidderminster had their border collie curled up at their feet, but that's allowed because you're eating at the bar.

You discovered it's the couple's first time on a canal, even though they've lived most of their lives a few miles from the Staffordshire & Worcestershire Canal Ⓦ. You asked why they're on this canal instead and they said they'd moved to be closer to the grandkids. Your meal was excellent and the service was excellent, even though you were in the bar because the restaurant was full and you had to give your order to the barman after looking at the menu chalked on a board.

Staffordshire & Worcestershire Canal Society
goo.gl/RgY2Z5

The 17th-century Hop Pole Inn

You stumbled back in the dark to the boat, using your smartphone as a light because you stupidly forgot to bring a flashlight. The smartphone's battery gave out halfway (because there were too many devices to charge and two few plugs on the boat), which was unfortunate because the pub is a short walk from the towpath along a one-lane road where cars whiz by at 40 miles per hour.

Back on the boat, you opened another bottle of wine and everyone got a little tipsy and you talked politics because everyone on the boat is of the same political persuasion. You actually had to talk because there's nothing else to do: no television or cellular reception. Everyone was a little hazy what day it was and no one knew the latest headlines. After thirty minutes, it was obvious everyone except you was tired, even though it was only half past eight. Someone's sleeping on the dinette double, however, so you couldn't linger and had to help put up the bed.

Most of the lights were soon extinguished because you worried about running down the batteries. Once in bed, your spouse was asleep before you. The only thing you could do was read, but long before 10 o'clock, you switched off your light.

The next morning you wake up an hour after sunrise, primarily because you went to sleep so early and secondarily because of the annoying duck outside your window. You have to stay in bed until you hear sounds of movement from the rest of the crew, however. Once the others are awake, you go into the kitchen to light the cooker, trying to remember the sequence to light a burner.

1. You have to turn the burner knob to the light position and then press and hold it in
2. Press the igniter switch (or apply a match or lighter) until the flame catches
3. Release the igniter switch but keep pressing the burner for the required amount of time (which varies). You're heating a flame safety device (a thermocouple or thermoelectric valve) that only permits gas to flow while the burner is lit. Once the flame goes out, the valve will close, preventing the buildup of gas in the cabin.
4. After a few seconds (again, the time varies depending on cooker model), you release the burner knob and can now adjust the flame intensity

It would be easy to figure this out if you were already caffeinated. Eventually you put the kettle on, but it takes forever for the water to boil (you may need to switch propane tanks) and you really wish the boat hire had provided an electric kettle. (Electric kettles and hair dryers can draw 2,000 watts, well beyond the capacity of the electrical system of most hire boats.)

After instant coffee (you'll discover on the last day the boat has a French press), you begin the daily engine checks and perhaps the checks you should have done the night before. After the dipstick, radiator and weed hatch have been inspected, you start the engine and cast off. Once underway, you remember to turn on the inverter to charge your cell phones and cameras and then realize it had been left on all night.

If you're fortunate, your first lock of the day is in a small town with a nearby bakery so someone can run out for scones and rolls. You hope to tour a stately home now owned by the National Trust by one o'clock, but there are five locks and two swing bridges before then. You decide to walk ahead on the towpath to stretch your legs and because two of the locks are in quick succession. Walking on the towpath you discover a boat that sells ice cream moored just before one of the busier and more picturesque locks. Luckily you have plenty of time to eat your ice cream because you walked so much faster than the boat can drive.

Today is the pleasantest day so far on the canal. If you're a beginner, maybe it's the third day of your mid-week break. Everyone's really starting to relax. Everyone's taken a turn at the tiller and all of you have some idea how to steer. Turning a lock is getting easier, although you dropped a windlass key somewhere and can't find it. Because it's fall, you've eaten your fill of the blackberries along the towpath. The leaves are just starting to turn but it's still warm during the day. You had rain the first day but now the sun is shining on this green and pleasant land.

Tomorrow is the day when you really have to put on the miles to make your return to the boat hire, and you realize a mid-week break is far too short. Already you're planning another canal trip, maybe even a ring route the next time.

What's provided, what's not

Narrowboat hire companies supply an impressive amount of what you'll need. Almost all boats will come with a full kitchen, including refrigerator, cook top (and probably an oven/grill) and sink. There's often a microwave oven and a full range of pots and pans, dishes, cups and silverware, plus the necessary washing up liquid, sponges and drying/tea towel. You'll even have toast racks (but no toaster) and eggcups, something most Americans will find amusing. We used the eggcups as shot glasses.

Groceries

You could bake a casserole, grill a steak or make a full English breakfast in a narrowboat galley. It might be difficult to bake a cake with only a whisk for mixing, but it can be done.

I suspect, however, that most people only get enough groceries for breakfast and lunch, because you'll want to eat at pubs along the way. On our trips, however, there were one or two nights when we were moored miles from the nearest hot meal.

It might seem anal, but create a shopping list of what you'll need before you pick up the boat. Agree on common items like sugar, bread, milk and butter (and agree on what you mean by those generic terms) and then agree on individual items so that you don't end up with a mysterious can of ox-tail soup no one can remember buying.

Fortunately there's almost always a grocery store either close to your boat hire or at a wharf along the canal. Long time boaters understandably might grumble at Tesco or Sainsbury's replacing an historic building, but you'll be glad of the convenience. Use Google maps or similar service to find the grocery stores along the canal.

Bed and bath

There may be a first-aid kit on board but don't count on it. You may want to stock up on cold remedies.

I recommend bringing your favorite cold medicines from home. Trying to divine the UK equivalent of Nyquil can be maddening.

Duvets and bottom sheets are provided for all the beds along with towels for all the listed passengers, but you probably won't have washcloths/facecloths. They're considered too personal an item and most UK travelers bring their own.

Things almost every boat will have

Diesel engine
DC-to-AC inverter
Windlasses
Mooring spikes and mallet
Mooring clamps
Pole and boat hook
Boarding ramp
Life ring (life preserver)
Water tank (at least a hundred gallons)
Hot water tank or calorifier, uses waste heat from the engine
Liquid propane gas tanks
Gas furnace, probably a boiler that heats water that is then piped to registers throughout the boat, may be tied into the hot water system
Fire extinguisher, fire blanket

Appliances, conveniences

TV, CD player, radio
and probably a Region 2 DVD player
Refrigerator
Kitchen sink
Cooker with oven and grill
Bathroom(s) with toilet, sink, shower and/or tub (with switch operated pump)

Kitchen

Plates (several sizes), bowls, coffee/tea cups, water glasses, wine glasses
Forks, knives, spoons
Fry pan
Fish slice (we'd call it a spatula or turner)
Several sauce pans
Colander
Bread box
Serving and cooking forks, spoons
Whisk
Carving knife, cutting board
Kettle
Tea pot
Tin and bottle opener, corkscrew
Tea towel, dish cloth, sponge, scouring pad, washing up liquid
Paper towels
Sufficient cups, plates, cutlery, etc., are provided for the maximum number of passengers the boat can accommodate. You'll also probably have a potato peeler, masher, oven gloves, egg cups, casserole dish, toast rack, butter dishes, sugar bowl, etc.
Waste bin (small)
Bucket, broom, mop, dust pan

Bed and bath

You'll have towels and bedding for how many people you told the boat hire will be aboard
12V hair dryer
Precious little toilet paper
Small waste bin

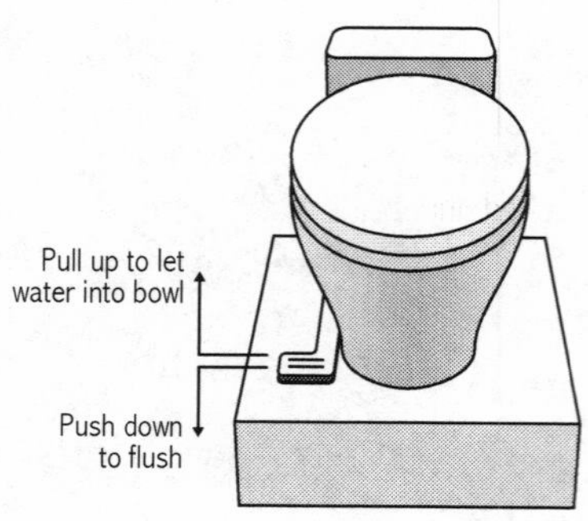

What may be provided (especially if you ask)

- Buoyancy aid (life vest)
- First-aid kit
- Waterproofs (rain gear)
- Umbrella

What's probably not provided

- Facial tissues
- Facecloths
- Hand soap

What you might want to bring

- Coat hangers
- Boat shoes (Crocs slip when wet)
- Toilet paper
- Facecloths
- 2-way radio
- Ear plugs
- Extension cord (to charge multiple devices)
- UK-to-US plug adapter
- Paper towels
- Facial tissues
- Hand soap
- Plastic storage bags
- Garbage bags
- Cooking oil (for the frying pan)
- Butter
- Sugar
- Coffee
- Tea
- Soft drinks
- Spirits
- Spices
- Breakfast food: cereal, rolls, scones
- Fruit: bananas, apples, grapes
- Jams, honey
- Condiments
- Cheese
- Crackers
- Cold remedies
- First-aid kit
- Clothesline
- Storage hooks

If you've not traveled outside the US, you may be unfamiliar with duvets, which replace the top or flat sheet most Americans use. The duvet has a removable cover that is washable. The duvet is not tucked under the bed. It's essentially a comforter. They are evil.

A narrowboat bathroom is understandably tiny and the toilet is usually perched uncomfortably high because of the sewage tank underneath. The flush lever is located at the base of the toilet. You pull up to let water into the bowl and push down to flush. There's usually a tiny sink and a tiny shower (one boat we booked had a tiny tub). There's a separate pump switch that drains the shower or tub. Gray water is dumped into the canal.

Don't expect the soaps and little bottles of shampoo and hand lotion that a hotel would provide. You can't use the hair dryer you brought, but instead have to be content with the provided anemic 12V device.

You'll probably have to get toilet paper at the first opportunity and paper towels to supplement the one provided hand towel.

Hacks and bodges

There are usually laundries convenient to the towpath (again, search online), but you still probably will have to wash clothes out in the sink (use the larger kitchen sink). Unless your boat has an airing cupboard (a small closet above the hot water tank or heating boiler), there's probably no place to hang wet clothes. I've finagled a clothesline with two suction cups to string across the shower or tub.

There's never enough storage space on a narrowboat, especially on a hire boat. Closets are small and scarce with never enough hangers. There are usually drawers underneath the bed or the dinette, but they're probably quite short because they pull out into the narrow hallway. You'll often find that if you lift up a mattress or cushion, however, that there's a plywood board underneath that can be lifted up for additional storage space. Be careful how you use this space, however, because you'll see the boat's wiring and plumbing and you don't want to damage what's there. There may be some water down there as well. Don't put anything there you'll forget. We've used it to store our empty luggage because we're unlikely to forget that when we leave the boat.

Shelf space is also at a premium. It's unlikely you'll stop at a DIY center to buy shelves, but you could probably find something like the adhesive hooks that can be removed without damaging paint or paneling. Even a small bag hung from a hook to give you a place to keep your glasses or cellphone would be a great convenience. I had everyone tearing up the boat for my camera because I didn't have a good place to store it.

There's never enough space in the tiny bathroom to hang up towels, but you'll notice there's usually a bar underneath each window to hold back the curtains (because the walls lean in), which is a perfect place to hang towels because there's usually a heat radiator there.

Dangers of the towpath

OK, really there are no dangers on the towpath apart from the occasional wobbly cyclist. If you are a cyclist, slow down when approaching people on the towpath and get off your bike if necessary. Boaters should not stretch lines across the towpath and pay attention when getting off the boat so you don't step in front of a bike.

There are no dangerous animals in the UK apart from the venomous adder (apparently a shy, timid snake), a bull in a field and loose dogs. Dogs are everywhere in the UK and so welcome in most places that it's a surprise to see a "No Dogs" sign. As a consequence, you'll also see lots of "No Dog Fouling" signs that seem to be widely ignored, leading to the most common danger on the towpath, stepping into a pile of dog poop.

If you fall into the canal, it's possible you might ingest enough water to be infected with leptospirosis bacteria (introduced into the water by rat urine) and develop Weil's disease. It's even possible to be infected by a cut, so it's a good idea to wash your hands after handling a line and to take a shower if you fall into the canal. If you develop flu-like symptoms, seek medical help and mention that you were recently on a canal.

The only real danger you'll regularly encounter is brushing up against stinging nettles. I've done so fre-

Stinging nettles (Urtica dioica) along a towpath

quently, but luckily I don't have much more reaction than a little redness and a little itchiness. The only proven remedies are antihistamines, either in a cream or as a pill or tablet (remember those cold remedies I suggested you bring?). Wash with soap and cold water to rinse off the irritant.

Pay toilets are very common in the UK. They're extremely clean and are serviced regularly. You can probably find one near a market square. It costs about 20-40p.

Services

You'll learn to keep an eye out for services as you travel, just as you would along a motorway, because it's even harder to turn a narrowboat around than your car. If you look carefully at a *Pearson's Canal Companion*, a *Nicholson's Guide* or a canal guide you download from the CRT or other waterways-related website, you can get a pretty good idea of what's along your canal.

The most important services are restrooms, water points, showers, groceries, laundries, electricity and waste disposal.

Restrooms

If you're lucky, there may be CRT restrooms and showers along your canal. You'll need a CRT key Ⓦ to access these. It's probably one of the keys hanging from the cork floater you were handed at the boat hire. (The other two keys are probably for the boat's ignition switch and the padlock on the rear hatch.)

Waterways
CRT key
goo.gl/tjRU1A

These keys can be bought from the CRT store for £7 and I think they make a great Christmas gift. It can be a pain to share the key that's attached to the cork floater (in case it falls in the water) and which also holds the ignition key and keys to the locks securing the hatches. A spare key can be a great convenience.

You might also find showers and even laundries at some CRT services. The showers are usually on a timer, providing water for a set time, and are free.

We take every advantage of every on-shore toilet to avoid filling up the waste tanks. We've also used CRT showers because showering on-board can be awkward and you needn't fear running out of water.

Water, electricity, waste

The key is also used to access the water points to fill the tank on your boat. You'll find posts like this along the canal, often near a lock or intersection. Never waste an opportunity to top up.

After unlocking the water point, you can drop down a hatch that will expose knobs or a lever to control the spouts on either side of the post. You'll connect to the outlets with the hose that you'll probably find in the gas locker in the front of the boat.

It's unlikely you'll be given a cable to connect the boat to an electric outlet on the towpath, but if you are, you can buy pre-paid cards from the CRT store in various denominations. Your boat manual will show you how to switch to mains power.

It's also unlikely that your boat hire will show you how to pump out waste, but you can ask. The canal trust also sells pump out cards, but it's really best if you stop at a marina and pay someone to do it for you. If your boat hire has multiple locations, they will probably pump you out for free at those locations. The pump out port on your boat is probably on the same side as the toilet.

Most narrowboats (and certainly most hired boats) have separate batteries to start the engine and to power the lights and kitchen appliances, so leaving the lights on and your device chargers plugged in all night won't prevent the engine from starting the next day. That said, draining the secondary batteries completely isn't a good idea and I'm sure is frowned on by your boat hire.

Yes, there's a bridge up ahead, the canal is turning to the right and you have no idea if another boat is coming. Remember to sound your horn.

How to steer a narrowboat

Few things are more daunting than when, after a thirty-minute lesson from your boat hire company, you're handed the tiller of a 65-foot-long iron-hulled narrowboat and told not to hit anything. You were told to move the tiller right when you want to move left and vice versa, but that's probably about the extent of the training you've been given regarding how to steer.

It might help if you've ever steered a fishing boat with an outboard motor, but that 20-foot aluminum craft is a much different beast than the 15-ton behemoth you now see stretching infinitely ahead of you from your vantage point at the tiller.

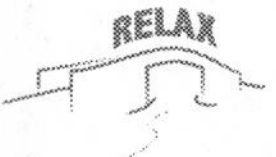

Relax! I know it's scary, but the reality is that 99% of your time on the water there's very little you can do that will cause any real damage because you're only moving at 2 or 3 miles per hour. You might be embarrassed and you might encourage the wrath of some feral boat people, but it's surprisingly difficult to cause any real damage or even any real inconvenience. And you will get better quite quickly.

Basic steering

The first, most basic steering advice to beginners is to push the tiller right to go left and push the tiller left to go right. This "opposite" advice never worked for me.

FIRST TIP: Point the tiller at the thing you DON'T want to hit. This is a handy tip for a beginner because for some reason the logic of turn right to go left doesn't make sense to the panicked brain.

Instead my husband offered the advice of doing something more mentally understandable, pointing the tiller at the thing you don't want to hit. But be patient, you will slowly move away from the thing you don't want to hit, which brings us to the second tip.

SECOND TIP: You have little control over steering if the propeller isn't in gear and turning. You may have to speed up to gain maneuverability, but if you're in imminent danger of colliding with something, it's better to put the throttle into full reverse.

Usually your first reaction when trying to avoid a collision is to pull back on the throttle, but as you reduce speed, you lose control and often you still hit. This does not, however, mean you should go full throttle all the time.

THIRD TIP: The boat turns about the middle of the boat, meaning the front of the boat might not hit the bridge, but the rear will.

A narrowboat handles very curiously because it's flat-bottomed and draws very little water. It's surprisingly maneuverable, but moving at such low speed, you have to anticipate your turns and wait for any movement of the tiller to have any effect. Once the boat does turn, it will continue to turn for some time. You'll quickly learn the side-to-side lazy small turns of the tiller that keeps the boat pointing in the right direction. What you don't want to do is move the tiller from side to side quickly because it will probably have little effect.

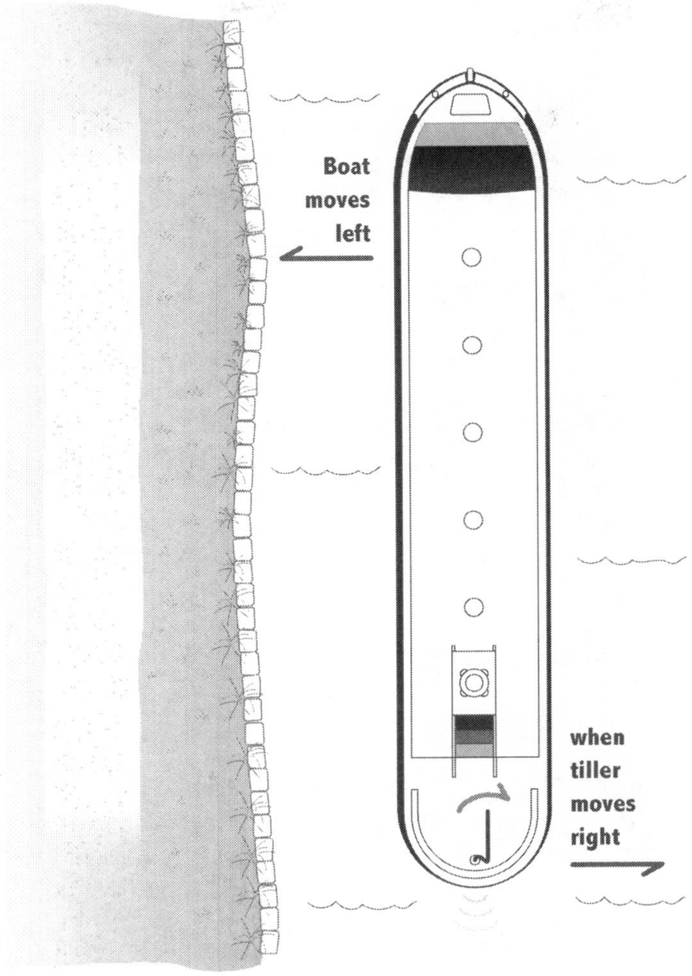

Boat moves left

when tiller moves right

When approaching a left-hand turn, you'll have to guess when you want to push the tiller right, knowing that the boat will turn about the middle, and obviously the advice is opposite when approaching a right-hand turn.

FOURTH TIP: You can steer the rear of the boat, sort of, by pushing the tiller hard in the direction you want the stern to go.

You'll often need to make quite sharp turns or multiple turns. When approaching a bridge, for instance, you'll often find it's not at 90° to the canal, and often the canal turns again on the other side of the bridge. The simple trick of aiming the tiller at the thing you don't want to hit may not be enough to avoid slamming into the bridge abutments (which is why the stone work of most bridges is often protected by wooden beams). Pushing the tiller right to make the front or bow of the boat go left also makes the rear or stern of the boat go right, and that might make the right end of the boat slam into an abutment.

You can steer the rear of the boat, however, by sharply pushing the tiller in the direction you want to move the stern — in other words opposite to the way you steer the front of the boat. So to move the front of the boat, you would push the tiller left to go right, but to move the stern of the boat, push the tiller hard right to go right.

Don't crowd the driver. The stern of the boat attracts people like the kitchen at a party, but sometimes the driver has to make sharp turns and you may find the end of the tiller in your stomach and / or get knocked off the boat.

And when I say hard right, I mean **push the tiller as far to the right as you can go**. This will affect the rear of the boat more than the front. You'll learn how long to keep the tiller hard right or left—usually it's not more than a second.

Turning the boat around

Turning the boat around in a winding hole is a daunting task for a beginner. Inevitably you'll have a crowd of other boaters laughing at you or offering advice. If you're lucky, your first winding hole will be in the middle of nowhere with earthen banks, so let's assume that will be [illegible] experience.

Everyone on the canal has advice for the poor chump steering the boat and at least half that advice is wrong. Learn to tell the difference.

As you approach, you'll want to cut power, even though it means you lose a lot of control. Anticipate before the middle of your boat approaches the middle of the winding hole and apply a short, full burst of reverse power. You don't need to stop the boat completely. Then, turn the tiller hard right or left and push the throttle forward. This should turn the boat around the middle. You also want to point the bow toward the softer bank (probably not the tow-path side). Ideally you don't want to hit the bank, but if you do, don't worry. With the bow against the bank, you'll find it's a lot easier to move the stern of the boat. Some winding holes are lined with stone, however, so avoid a full speed crash.

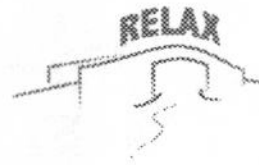

Your first winding hole will seem like a slow-motion nightmare, but as long as you're not in a marina surrounded by moored boats, it's not that difficult.

To avoid hitting the bank, apply short, full bursts of reverse with the tiller in line with the boat. Then continue to steer the stern of the boat, applying short bursts of forward thrust and pushing the tiller hard right to move the stern right and hard left to move the stern left.

Winding holes are rarely round. They're often little more than a wider part of the canal and sometimes they have one or two straight sides, making a sort of triangle. Winding holes are sometimes marked with the size of boat that can successfully turn around.

A bow thruster is little more than a propeller or propellers mounted in a tube that pierces the front of the boat from left to right. The propeller(s) are powered by electric motors or hydraulically driven.

Bow thrusters/wheel steering

It's unlikely you'll hire a boat with bow thrusters, but they are available on some luxury boats. I've encountered them once at a boat hire on the Monmouthshire & Brecon Canal, but the rental cost proved prohibitive. If

Feral boat people

I've mentioned the feral boat people a few times without explaining who they are and what threat they pose to you, the newbie narrowboater. Here's what you need to know: Ferals are a subset of the mostly well-adjusted, happy liveaboards you meet on the water, but over time they've become grouchy and sullen. Previously they might have covered the roofs of their boats with cheerful canal art water cans and beds of flowers, but now their boats are something you want to hurry past. Some canals and certain stretches of canals are more attractive to ferals and you will see them in higher concentrations. You'll recognize ferals when you see:

- Unusual boats. Ferals love to inhabit oil rig survival pods, original working narrowboats or narrowboats done up as submarines. Boats are either unusually long or incredibly short.
- No exposed roof. It's covered with wheelbarrows, dead plants, bicycles, solar panels, windmills, lumber, tires, etc.
- You can't see into the windows because all the dirty curtains are closed or the boat is jam packed with stuff or they're obscured with hand-lettered signs such as "Would you pour boiling water on your baby? Slow Down!" or "Save the Badgers!"
- What appears to be an abandoned boat until you see a curtain twitch or if you're unwise enough to rock their boat with your wake or God forbid you crash into their boat. Then they erupt from their boat calling you a "festering gob" or a "gormless sod."

Ferals are mostly harmless, except to your *sang-froid*. You might have been whistling a happy tune, putting down the canal without a care in the world, congratulating yourself for finally figuring out how to steer. Then you get yelled at to "Slow Down!" because in your oblivious happiness you had failed to slow for their moored boat. They're correct for chastising you, of course, but was it really necessary for them to shoot those fire arrows at your boat and to jump up in down in their ritual war chant?

you're traveling alone a bow thruster would be handy to push off the front of a boat when leaving a mooring.

Similarly, you might hire a boat with a steering wheel, where turning the wheel right makes the boat go right, but it's unlikely. Searching for these sort of extra features would limit the canals you can travel.

Turning in a marina

This is undoubtedly a high-stress situation, and the only solace I can offer is that it's a different kind of stress than most of us have to contend with in our day-to-day lives. A mistake on the canal usually just means you've hit a moored boat and an irritable head will pop out and curse you with a charming English (or Welsh or Cornish or Scottish or Irish) accent.

Don't be afraid to apply full reverse thrust. It's a little alarming to see the water churning behind you, but it takes quite a lot to reverse the momentum of the boat.

Of course if you make a mistake on the canal, remember that you'll probably see the witnesses to your disaster again and again if they are traveling the same direction as you. They may be waiting for you at the next lock or sitting at the next table at the pub that night. Thus it pays to be polite to people on the canal.

AVOID pushing your boat away from another boat by placing the pole against the superstructure—the upper, probably prettily painted part—of that boat.

Actually, you'll find most people want to offer you friendly advice. True, half that advice is wrong, but generally it's kindly meant. Often there will be a concerned boat owner who's happy to take your bow line and guide your boat away from his boat. The reality is, however, that you will hit other boats. Be prepared to use the pole on your boat to push your boat away.

Turning in a marina on a windy day

Abandon all hope of a pleasant experience when trying to turn a boat on a windy day in a marina. The only advice I can offer is to try to gauge the direction of the wind and know that when your boat is perpendicular to the wind, you will be pushed away and plan your turn appropriately.

Try to keep facing forward when reversing. It's very easy to accidentally put the boat in reverse when you meant to go forward because you're now facing the rear of the boat. It's very easy to get turned around in a lock, causing you to ram the gate you're trying to avoid.

Reverse

Realistically there's only one direction you can steer a boat in reverse and that direction is straight back. You will need to get the boat pointed in the proper direction with forward momentum and then apply reverse thrust and hope you've got the boat pointed in the right direction. Keep the tiller in line with the boat and then pray to the canal gods.

Of course that never works and you will often find the boat veering right or left. Your best bet then is apply a short burst of forward throttle and push the tiller right to turn the front of the boat left and push the tiller left to go right; or to move the stern of the boat, push the tiller hard right to move the stern right or hard left to move it left. Again, don't be afraid to churn water during these maneuvers.

Buy cheap, two-way radios for your trip. They will work as intercoms from your spotters in the bow to the driver in the stern. You can also use them when sending people ahead to check the status of a lock or when to enter a tunnel.

Communication

The one concept that never seems to sink in for even the most experienced boaters is that shouting really doesn't work. The people in the front of the boat can hear the people in the back, but the people in the back can't hear the people in the front (because of the engine). And so a lot of only half-understood conversations pass back and forth while the boat inexorably crashes into a helpless kayaker.

Realistically, however, there are only a few important messages that need to be passed between the spotters in the bow and the driver in the stern: Another boat is approaching, a bridge or tunnel is ahead, slow down, stop and all clear. A few simple arm and hand gestures will convey all that. You might not like the ones suggested here, so come up with your own agreed upon gestures (I still haven't come up with any for swing bridges, tunnels and moor here) and try to repair the American reputation for being loud.

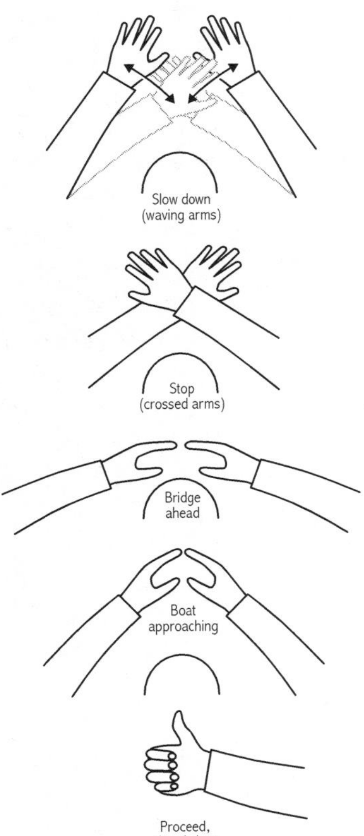

So You've Run Aground

You know intellectually that running aground is no big deal. You know that feral boat people are not going to strip your boat, take your women (or men) and sell them into slavery. You know your boat won't be dashed against the rocks. And yet there are few things on the water that make you feel so helpless.

What really makes you feel like a pillock is that your first reaction when you bottomed out was to push the throttle. Now the propeller is churning water, everyone on the boat is asking what's going on and the feral boat people are yelling at you not to leave a wake.

First, take your hand off the throttle. You ran into something. Increasing the throttle is only driving the boat farther into the mud, sand, weeds or some combination thereof.

Second, tell everyone on the boat (including you) to **move to the other side of the boat**. Right now, everyone is to one side of the boat, looking at the bank on which you're caught. The other side of the boat is probably free. Moving to the other side will lift the side of the boat that's stuck.

It's unlikely to happen on a narrowboat, but pleasure craft occasionally roll over when everyone is on side of the boat, so this advice should be followed cautiously on a small boat (and certainly on any boat with a keel).

Third, **put the throttle in reverse** and don't be afraid to churn water, even if does draw more attention. It is the front of the boat that's caught, so it makes sense to back out.

You're probably free now, but if not:

Fourth, get out the pole. I used to think every problem could be solved with the pole because of Archimedes' "Give me a lever long enough and a place to stand and I can move the Earth" gag, but that lever won't work if you're pushing it into a patch of muddy weeds, or if the lever isn't long enough. But if you've run aground against the towpath side, then the lever might be long enough and the ground firm enough.

You can also try having everyone get off the boat and thus lightening it. Obviously this is most easily done if you've run aground on the towpath side. See if you can push off the boat with the pole, but keep a grip on the center line.

Fifth, and let's hope it doesn't come to this, you may need to **throw a line to the other bank** and have the rest of your crew pull it free. If you've run aground against a weed-choked bank with grown over trees and no one can get off, you'll need to enlist the help of other boaters, hikers or cyclists.

Running the stern aground

This isn't as common as running the bow aground, but it can happen, as my husband reminded me. If you've just made a tight turn around a bend in the canal, the stern of your boat might have caught on weeds, mud or sand. If you suspect there are a lot of weeds, then try remedies other than using the throttle: moving the crew to the other side or to the front of the boat, getting off the boat or pushing with the pole.

Don't put the throttle in reverse, you'll just drive the stern farther into the obstruction. Instead, point the tiller away from where the boat is caught and apply forward throttle. If you hear banging and scraping, however, stop immediately. You don't want to damage the propeller.

If you've had to use the throttle where there are weeds, then inspect the weed hatch afterward and clear the propeller shaft if needed.

To avoid running aground, try to keep to the center of the canal as much as possible, but remember that boats pass on the right. Rather than being forced to pass another boat on the right when you suspect there are weeds, tree roots or mud, slow down and let the other boat pass where there is more room.

I suppose there is a possibility you might have run aground in the center of the canal because of a submerged tree trunk or shopping cart (perhaps on an urban canal). Some variation of one of these techniques should work. As far as I know, there are no narrowboats permanently stuck in the middle of any canals, the crew reduced to moldering skeletons.

There are often moments of transcendent beauty along a canal, where the sky, the trees and the water melt together like an impressionist painting. My apologies if you're seeing these pictures in the black-and-white paperback edition.

Blackberry bushes are very common along towpaths and a late summer or early fall boating trip should ensure encountering a plentiful harvest.

Mooring

It's odd, but your boating adventure becomes a little more adventurous when you've stopped moving. You really can't get into much trouble while putting along the canal, but a bad mooring can ruin your day. Let's look at the two types of moorings a typical holiday canal cruiser encounters and how to improve the experience.

DANGER! It can be dangerous to moor a still moving boat because it's easy to trap a hand between a line and a bollard or ring. You could also weaken the bollard or ring and also stress your line.

A quick mooring

While waiting in line at a lock or at a water point, you will only have to moor for a brief time and consequently the list of things you need to bear in mind is mercifully short.

It's best to approach the towpath or bank at an angle and slowly. Put the throttle in reverse briefly to almost stop the boat. A person in the front of the boat will step

Quick mooring rules

- Moor on the towpath side whenever possible
- Don't moor immediately before or after a bridge, lock, water point, weir, slipway, junction or bend of the canal. Don't moor such that you block the approach to the bridge, lock, etc.
- Whenever possible, moor where there are mooring rings or bollards
- Don't block the towpath with mooring lines
- Don't moor where prohibited—duh!

---

off with a mooring line and secure the boat to a mooring ring or bollard.

DANGER!

Avoid the temptation to jump off the boat as you could easily slip and fall. Also, don't try to slow the boat when approaching the bank by putting out your foot. That's a good way to break a leg.

To get the stern of the boat close to the towpath or pier, push the tiller hard left to move the stern left or hard right to move the stern right, and apply a little forward throttle. Once the boat has stopped and is against the towpath, put the throttle in neutral. If it's a two-person boat, the driver will step off and run a line to the towpath and then back to the boat, tying it off on a bitt or cleat on the stern.

Whenever possible, run lines back to the boat. It will allow you to untie while on the boat and uses up a lot of the extra line that you would otherwise trip over.

Secure lines to bollards or rings with a round turn (two loops). You don't have to tie up as long as mooring lines are attended, but pay attention when moored at the lower end of a lock. The outflow from the lock might pull the boat away from its mooring.

The front and stern lines should extend from the

Mooring approach

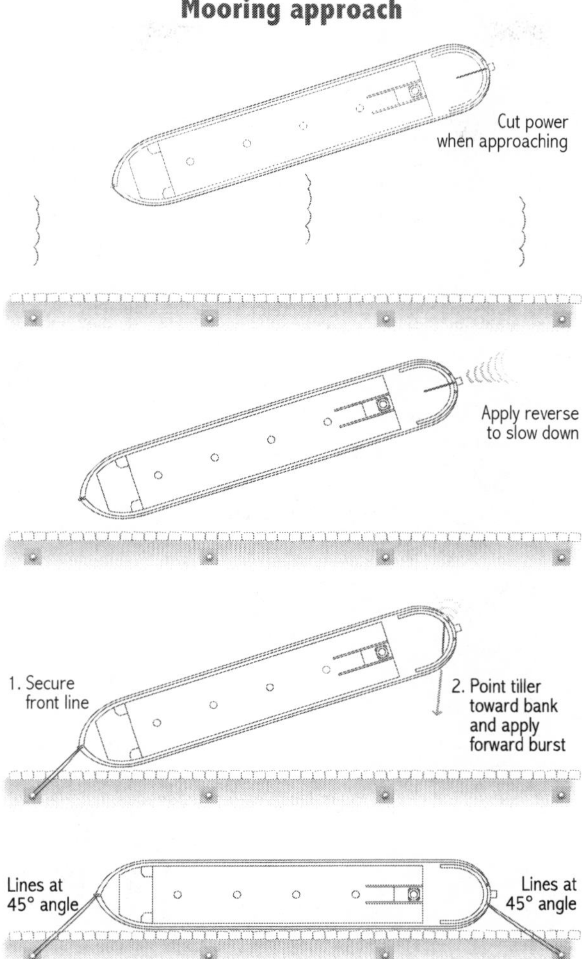

boat at a roughly 45° angle. You shouldn't use the center line for mooring because it tilts the boat, but for mooring while waiting at a lock while the boat is otherwise attended, it's OK.

To leave a mooring, someone can push off the front of the boat and step back onboard once the boat is moving. It doesn't take much to move the boat away from the towpath or bank unless there's a wind or other current keeping the boat there.

Leaving a tight mooring

Often you'll need to leave a mooring when there are boats in front of and behind yours. If you don't have someone to push off the bow, then swing out the stern of the boat by pointing the tiller sharply away from the bank and apply forward throttle. Once the stern is clear of the boat behind you, apply reverse throttle until you have room to maneuver the front of the boat.

Overnight mooring

An overnight mooring requires a little more attention to detail. All the quick mooring rules apply, but in addition, be on the lookout for signs indicating whether you *can* moor, are *prohibited* from mooring or informing you *how long* you can moor.

The canal guide you downloaded or your *Pearson's* or *Nicholson's* guides will have similar symbols informing you of mooring permissions and restrictions, but the general rule still applies that you can moor anywhere along the towpath that is not otherwise prohibited.

The longest you can moor in one spot is 14 days. Some liveaboards who have a cruising license must pull up stakes every two weeks and travel to another mooring.

Some free moorings are better than others, of course. The best moorings have bollards or rings, second best has the horizontal metal rails that allow use of piling hooks, and least favored are unlined rough banks choked with reeds, nettles and silt. You'll recognize the unfavored moorings while desperately searching for a spot for the night when you ask, "I wonder why nobody has moored along this stretch?" A rough bank often means it's difficult to tie up close and you'll need the gangplank to get ashore.

Some canals have reserved public moorings that can be claimed by paying at some designated place, and sometimes these include water points and power. It can

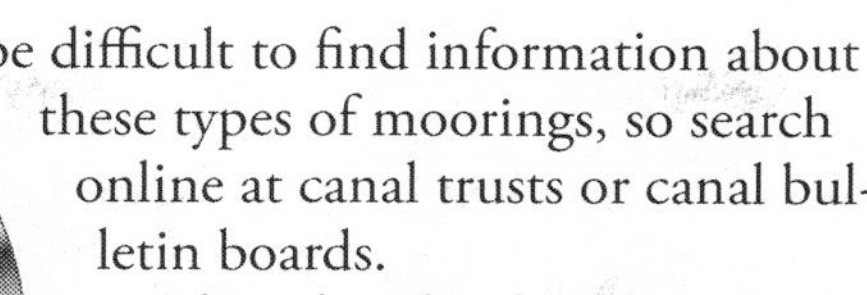

be difficult to find information about these types of moorings, so search online at canal trusts or canal bulletin boards.

The piling hooks (also called nappy pins) provided with your boat (unless the canal you're traveling has no piling rails) are hooked through the rail/girder that runs along the top of the corrugated metal pilings. (It's very easy to drop these into the canal, by the way.) You just run your mooring line through the ring and back to the boat if possible.

Occasionally you'll need to use mooring spikes and hopefully they will provide spikes with rings to attach a line. Here are some truths about mooring spikes: The ends are never sharp and the spikes are never straight and they're never long enough. Drive spikes into the ground at an angle, the ends pointing away from the boat. Your boat will have a mallet to drive them into the ground. Drive a spike in only about three-quarters of its length.

Share a mooring ring or bollard with other boats when practical, especially at a popular mooring

Don't drive spikes too close to the edge of the bank, because they'll pull loose and weaken the bank. Don't drive them in the towpath. Don't tie the boat tightly to the spikes because any movement of the boat (caused by a passing boat) will loosen the spikes. Check your spikes frequently and before going to sleep. Tie a flag of some sort (a bandanna or grocery/carrier bag) to the spike to warn passers-by.

Mooring on rivers

Mooring on a river is a little more complicated because you should moor with the front of the boat

Cast adrift

Mooring lines can come undone for any number of reasons. On our 2015 Wales trip, we left behind with the boat Jim (our friend Lee's brother who was suffering from a head cold) when we walked from our mooring to the town of Llangollen, about 2½ miles. We were touring a historic house when we got a call from Jim saying the boat was adrift in the canal. We'd hoped to eat lunch in Llangollen before returning, but we hurried back to the boat (although we did stop for pasties to eat while walking). When we returned, we found the boat moored to a tree and then learned of Jim's adventure. He relates:

"I was either reading, napping, or both, when I was startled by the sound of a narrowboat horn. What I discovered was that the narrowboat (all 65 feet) was lying near straight across the canal with only its bow line still attached to the mooring pin. It was blocking the entire canal which in turn caused a narrowboat attempting to pass, to come to a stop and sound its horn."

Jim eventually leapt to the towpath with the centerline of the boat and with the help of a passerby tied the boat to a bench and later to a tree. (The stern mooring pin had fallen into the canal and he was unable to retrieve it.) Unfortunately the centerline crossed the towpath about knee height, so Jim removed the centerline and tied it to the bowline and with the added length, was able to lower the line to ground level.

Jim has had time to reflect what went wrong: "I do remember that we tied up along a straight stretch of the canal, with a narrow strip of grass between the edge of the canal and a concrete or paved walkway. The ground was wet, and upon recollection perhaps a little soft. Thinking back, I suspect we did not take into account the wet ground and the relatively higher speed of the other boats, along the straight stretch of the canal which can rock the boat and alternately tighten and loosen the tension on the mooring line."

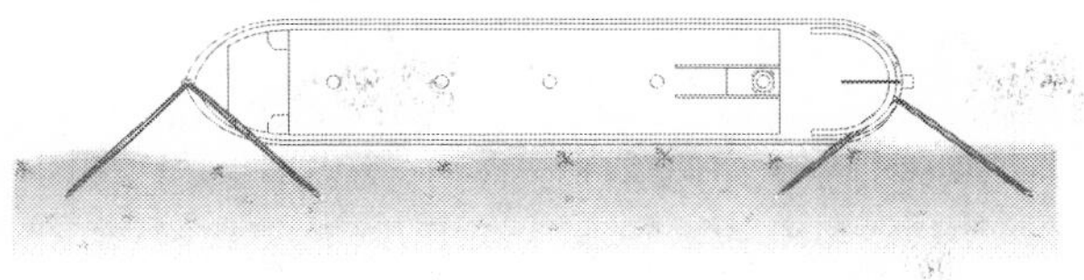

When mooring on a river, you'll need extra lines front and back to keep the current from pulling out your mooring pins

pointing into the current. (You should also moor facing into a strong wind.) That means you may have to turn the boat around.

You may also need to add extra lines to secure your boat and you should ensure you have extra lines if planning to take your hire narrowboat on a river. Always tell your boat hire if you plan to take your boat on a river to make sure they provide you an anchor and extra lines.

When mooring on a river (with the boat pointing upstream), tie the bow line first. When leaving a mooring, release the stern line first.

Mooring on tidal rivers

It's even more important not to moor against a bank on a tidal river for any length of time. The water may rise and fall considerably and you might find the boat hanging from its ropes. Always moor at a harbor or marina overnight on tidal rivers.

Although restrictions have relaxed, hired narrowboats are still not allowed on the Thames from Brentford to Limehouse, where the tidal river can create choppy and fast-flowing water

Stream advisories

You should check with the appropriate authorities what stream conditions are like before venturing onto rivers. A quick call to a phone number or a visit to a website will advise whether it's safe to venture out (See "Thames stream advisories" on page 116).

Mooring in a marina/pre-booked moorings

I'm notoriously cheap and normally wouldn't think of paying for a mooring, but there are advantages of knowing that however late you arrive, you have a mooring waiting for you. Unfortunately the short-term booking at most marinas is monthly, so unless you're planning a very long narrowboat vacation without intending to go very far, it's not very cost effective. Nevertheless, I occasionally find marinas with daily rates.

Pre-booked moorings in London
goo.gl/ck92bT

Ignoring marinas, there are some moorings that can be reserved for short or overnight stays, but information on these are usually hard to find and often require emails or phone calls to secure. For instance the Canal & River Trust has berths in Llangollen, but you'll have to show up in person at Llangollen Wharf (home of the horse-drawn boats) to get one for that day. The CRT also has short-term mooring in London Ⓦ (in Little Venice).

Avon Navigation Trust
goo.gl/7ZX8d2

There are also moorings provided by trusts and other navigation authorities, although these usually can't be pre-booked. The Avon Navigation Trust Ⓦ, which administers the River Avon that flows beside Shakespeare's home town, marks its moorings with light blue posts to differentiate them from private moorings.

I'm afraid the long and the short of it is getting a marina or pre-booked mooring will require a lot of research and a lot of luck.

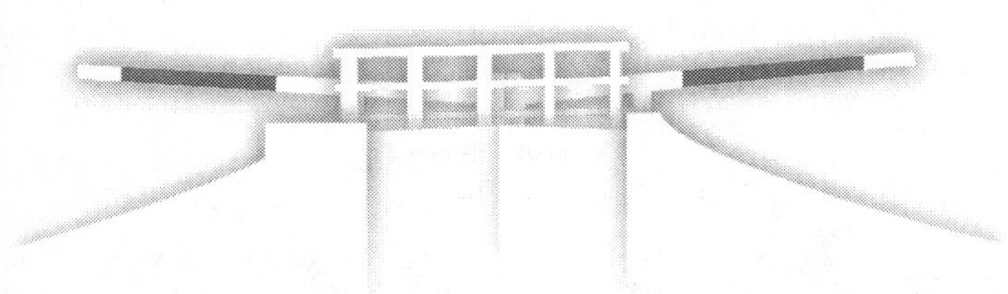

Locks, bridges and tunnels

Turning a lock is a daunting task for beginning narrowboaters for several reasons: it is the one canal task that can cause serious damage or injury; despite being a fundamentally simple technology, it can be difficult to understand how it works; and most significantly, it exposes a beginner to ridicule. Unless you have enormous self-confidence, you will approach your first lock fearing the laughter of children and the scorn of your fellow boaters.

People who watch canal activity are called gongoozlers (especially if they offer useless advice). Gongoozling is similar to trainspotting (what railroad train watching is called in the UK).

One way to avoid looking stupid is to watch other boaters turn a lock and see how it's done beforehand. Perhaps you can schedule your vacation so that you can spend a day on the canal before you book the boat. Most people on the canals are happy to talk and offer advice to beginners, as long as you don't get in the way.

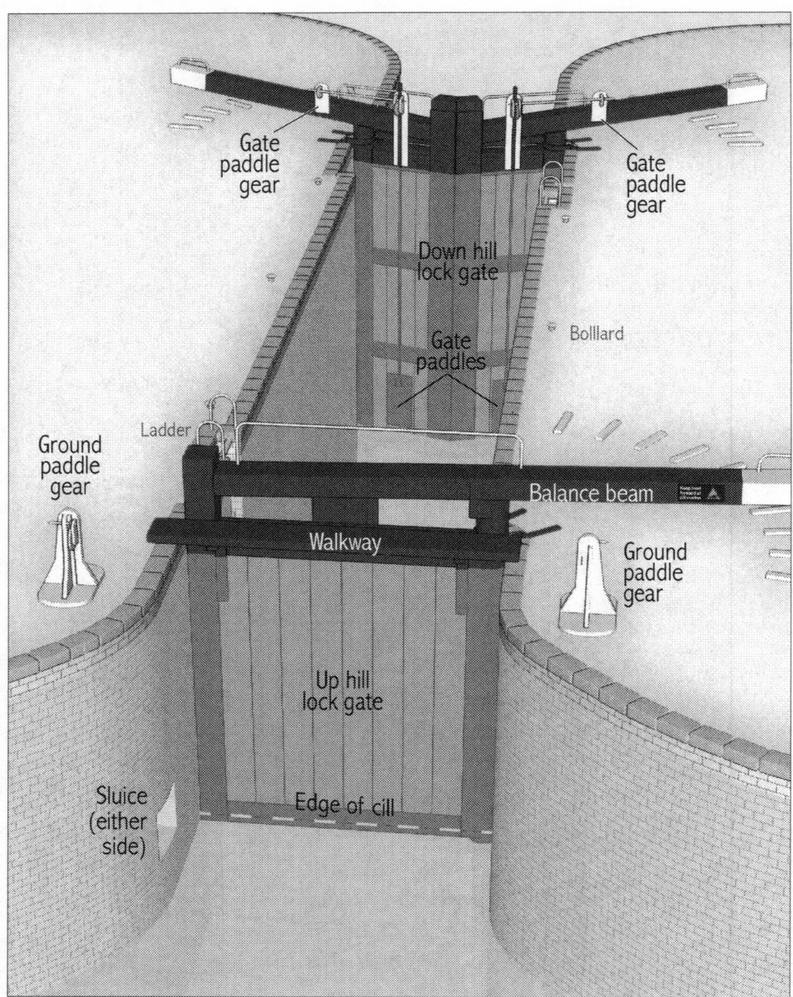

How a lock works

Because it's a pretty simple technology, canal locks haven't changed much in hundreds of years. A lock on the Panama Canal works on much the same principles as a lock on the Leicester Canal. Both canals employ pound locks, pound referring to the water between locks.

For such a simple technology, however, there is quite a variety of locks on the canals. There are single-boat

Raise pawl to lower paddle

locks, double-width locks and the massive locks on the Thames. Boaters turn most locks themselves, manually turning a windlass to raise paddles, but some are overseen by lock keepers, some are operated by lock keepers and some are operated by electrical motors controlled by boaters or lockkeepers. There are flights of locks, staircase locks, guillotine locks and even diamond locks (but precious few of those).

Water is generally allowed into the lock (on the uphill or higher side) via *sluices* that are built into the banks of the lock. Water is generally let out of the lock (on the downhill side) via openings in the gates or by sluices built into the bank, just as on the uphill side. In either case, the openings in the gates or the sluices are controlled by *paddles*. (In actual practice, you'll see many combinations of gate and ground paddles.)

Ground paddle gear

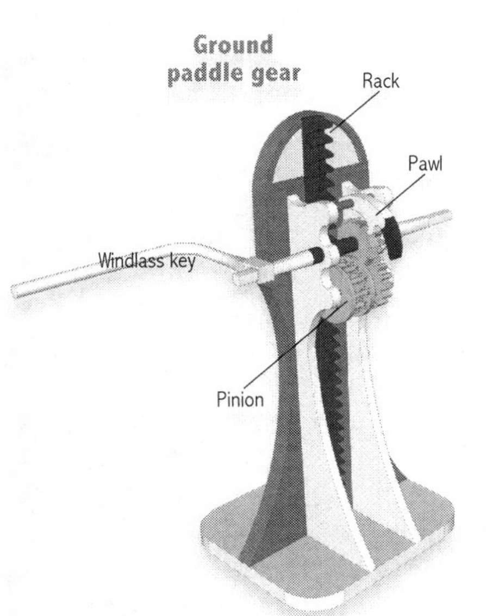

The paddle is connected to a metal rod which in turn is connected to a metal-toothed bar or *rack*. The rack (and the paddle) is pulled up or down by the *pinion*, which is a round, toothed gear that meshes with the teeth on the rack. The pinion is turned by a *windlass* crank (also called a lock key), which is inserted over a spindle or shaft.

To prevent the rack and the paddle from dropping back down once the windlass key is removed, there is a *pawl* or metal hook that works against the teeth of a gear (the *ratchet*) that's on the spindle. To crank the paddles back down, the pawl must be disengaged by pulling it away from the gear. In order to raise the pawl, you'll have to slightly turn the windlass key in the opposite direction that the teeth on the ratchet are pointing.

Leonardo da Vinci invented the mitered lock gate. Most gates are angled 18° to approximate an arch. Mitered gates point uphill and the pressure of the water keeps them shut.

The balance beams attached to the gates are very long for two reasons—to make a longer lever for closing the very heavy gates and to counter-balance the weight of the gate itself. Lock gates can hardly be said to be hinged. They fit into a rounded groove in the walls of the lock chamber, held in place by relatively thin metal straps and the pressure of the water. Essentially the oak gates float in the water.

The gates of the lock are opened by pushing the attached *balance beams*. To help a boater push against the beam, there are usually raised bricks set in the ground to provide footing while pushing or pulling the beams.

The uphill gates open outward, into the canal. The downhill gates open inward, into the lock chamber.

There is a *cill*—a masonry or concrete shelf—just inside the uphill lock or gate. The gate (or gates) shuts against the cill. When the lock chamber is filled, a boat entering the lock rides over the cill when going downhill. There is a warning on the walls of the lock chamber to indicate the edge of the cill.

Don't allow the rear of the boat to be caught on the cill while draining water from the pound. This is a relatively short cill.

There are usually ladders built into the side of the lock chamber. They're narrow and slippery and primarily there for the convenience of a boat crewed by one person, to let that person go up to open or close paddles and gates or go down to drive the boat out of the lock. A person who falls into a lock can also climb the ladder to safety.

There are either bollards or mooring rings on either side of the lock chamber, again chiefly for the convenience of one-person boats, to keep the boat from drifting too close to the cill by wrapping the center line around one of the bollards.

At the downhill end, water is let out of the lock either through sluices in the banks or paddles in the gates. If there are gate paddles, the spindle or shaft that turns the pinion (which raises the rack and the attached paddle) runs along the balance beam you push to open and close the gate.

Usually there's a walkway that runs along the top of the outside face of the downhill gate. You cross the lock on that narrow platform, keeping a hand on the railing that is attached to the beam. There's usually a similar platform on the uphill gate. It can be a little unnerving crossing the lock the first time and you'll be thankful for the non-slip surface on the platform. Occasionally there's a more substantial bridge on the downhill side.

Understand the principles of hydrodynamics, i.e. water flows downhill

A lock works because water wants to go downhill. By controlling the flow of water with two lock gates and with a means to let water in or out, a boat can go either up or down. When a boat enters a lock, the gate closest to the boat must be open and the gate farthest away must be closed. Water must then be let out if the boat is going down or let in if the boat is going uphill. Then the position of the gates is reversed.

Even in the UK, water is not an inexhaustible commodity and occasional droughts have forced the closure of some canals. It's important to close gates and paddles to prevent water loss.

A lock also works because there is an "inexhaustible" supply of water feeding the canal at its highest points. That's one reason canals usually follow river courses—to have a steady water source. You'll also find pumping stations and reservoirs near these high points. (The other reason canals follow rivers is that rivers have already excavated a nearly level path the canal can use. Later railroads would take advantage of the same course the canals took, sometimes filling the canal for railway beds.)

When going downhill, a lock is in your favor if the pound or lock chamber is already filled. When going uphill, a lock is in your favor if the lock chamber is empty.

Turning a lock

Let's pretend you have a crew of four, which is the ideal number for a beginner boat crew—one person to drive the boat, one person at the front of the boat to handle the bow line and two people to work the paddles and gates.

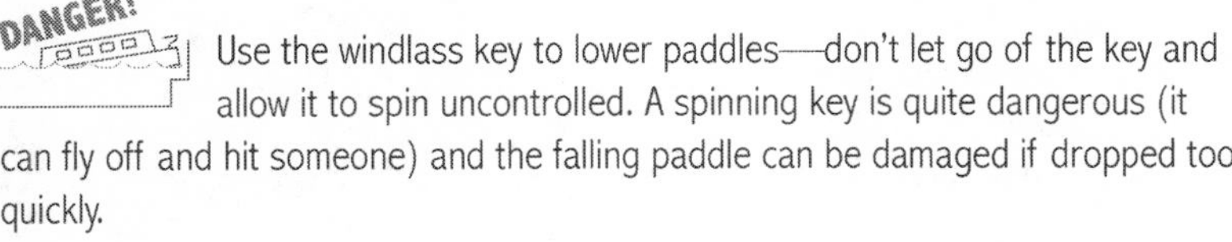

Use the windlass key to lower paddles—don't let go of the key and allow it to spin uncontrolled. A spinning key is quite dangerous (it can fly off and hit someone) and the falling paddle can be damaged if dropped too quickly.

The towpath bank on either side in front of a lock is usually lined with masonry or timber and there are bollards or mooring rings to secure a boat (see the mooring chapter.) The driver should nose into the towpath bank and let a person in the bow step out and secure the boat with the front line. One or both of the lock turners should go ahead to see whether the lock is set in your favor, if there's traffic in the other direction and how many boats are in the queue.

If you're moored downhill of a lock that is emptying, be aware that the flow of water can move your boat back. Keep a tight hand on any lines and when available, pass your rope through a mooring ring or around a bollard. The boat driver should be ready to apply some throttle to keep the boat against the towpath or avoid banging into another boat.

If the lock is in your favor, the lock turners may need to open gates and check to see if the ground or gate

Going Downhill

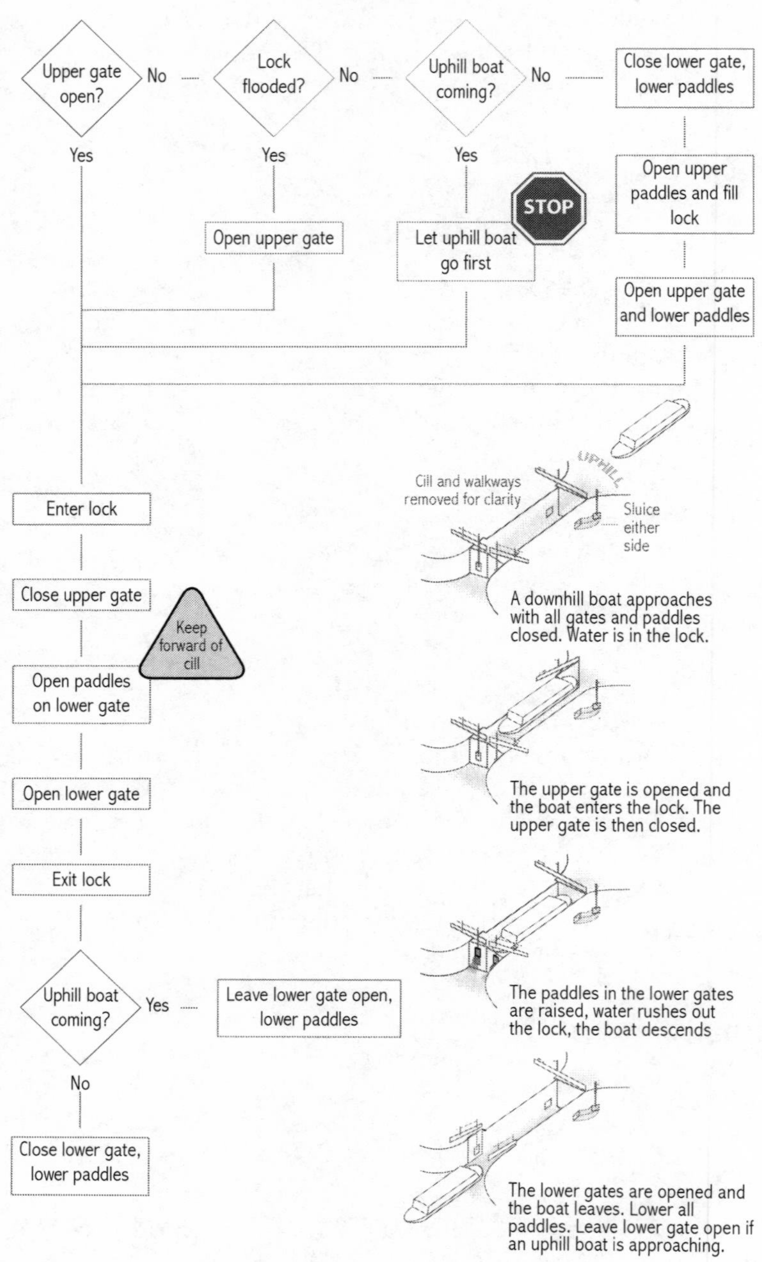

A downhill boat approaches with all gates and paddles closed. Water is in the lock.

The upper gate is opened and the boat enters the lock. The upper gate is then closed.

The paddles in the lower gates are raised, water rushes out the lock, the boat descends

The lower gates are opened and the boat leaves. Lower all paddles. Leave lower gate open if an uphill boat is approaching.

Going Uphill

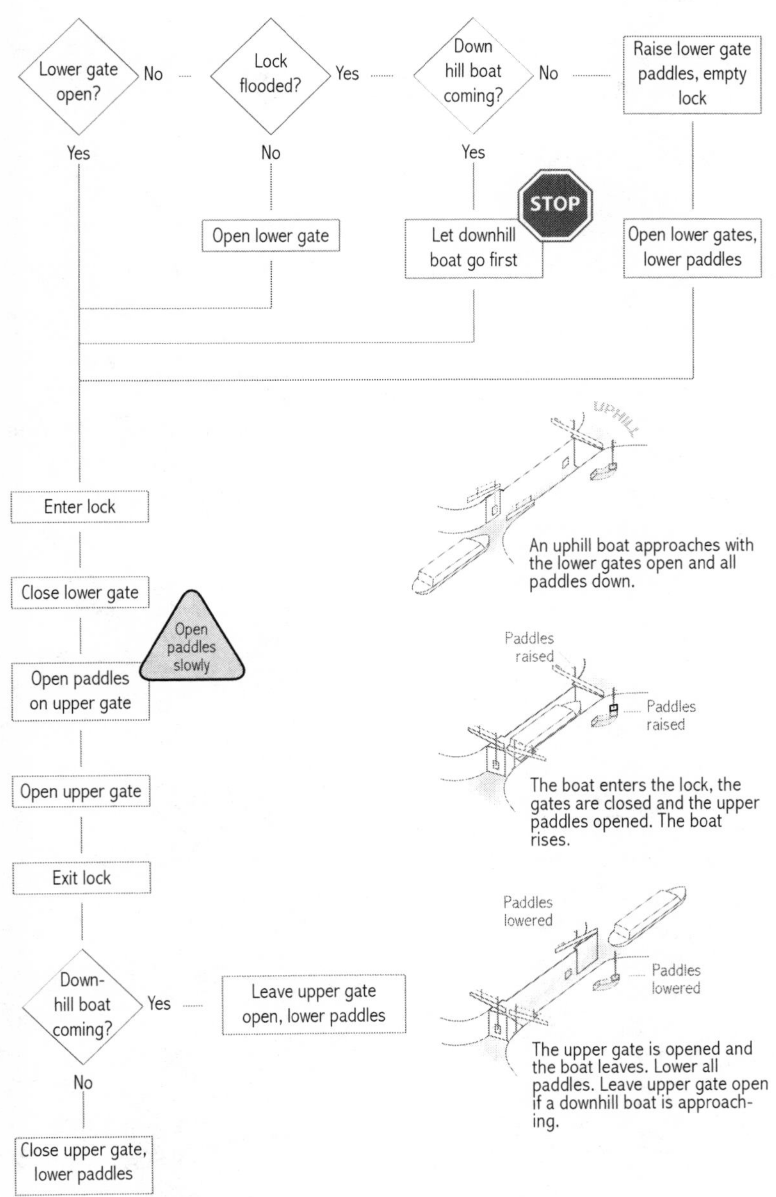

An uphill boat approaches with the lower gates open and all paddles down.

The boat enters the lock, the gates are closed and the upper paddles opened. The boat rises.

The upper gate is opened and the boat leaves. Lower all paddles. Leave upper gate open if a downhill boat is approach-ing.

paddles are lowered. If the lock isn't in your favor, the lock turners will need to flood or drain the lock chamber before opening the gates.

Once the lock is set, the lock turners will signal to the boat to come ahead. The bow person will release the forward line, push the boat off, get on board and the driver will proceed into the lock.

Once through the lock, the driver will again nose into the towpath. The person in the bow will step out and secure the boat until the lock turners are back on board. Then the bow person will release the boat, push off and get on board.

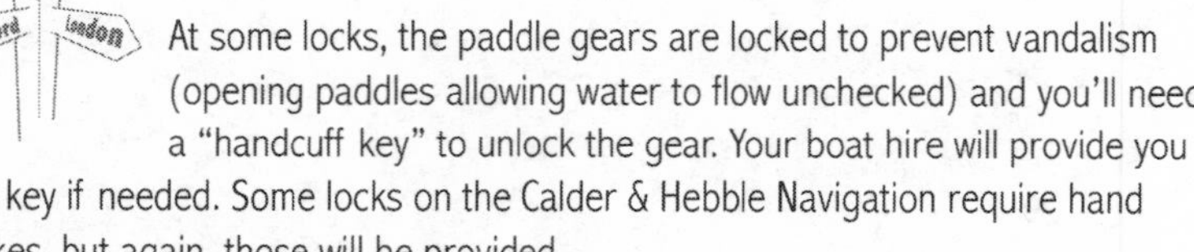

At some locks, the paddle gears are locked to prevent vandalism (opening paddles allowing water to flow unchecked) and you'll need a "handcuff key" to unlock the gear. Your boat hire will provide you the key if needed. Some locks on the Calder & Hebble Navigation require hand spikes, but again, those will be provided.

Smaller crews

A three-person crew works much the same way. Only one lock turner is required—it just goes faster with two to raise and lower paddles.

A two-person crew requires a little more hustle. The bow person will secure the boat until the driver can get off and hold the boat in place with the center line. The bow person then becomes the lock turner, raising or lowering water and opening gates as necessary. After the boat leaves the lock, it can be a little more difficult for the lock turner to get back on the boat. The driver can either throw the center line to the person on the towpath or they can try to get on from the bow. If the former, leave the center line easily accessible.

Turning paddle gears with a windlass key sometimes requires a great deal of effort. A ratcheted windlass makes the task much easier. Unfortunately you'd probably have to buy it, have it shipped to you and then include it in your carry-on luggage.

Going it alone

Going It Alone
goo.gl/zfN2wK

It's not in the scope of this book to address turning a lock by yourself, but it's often done (I've never done it). The two difficulties are climbing up or down the ladders and keeping the boat away from the gates while draining or filling the lock chamber. That's where the center line and the bollards along the lock banks are useful. If you are determined to go it alone, the Inland Waterways Assocation offers Colin Edmondson's pamphlet appropriately named *Going it Alone*Ⓦ.

Types of locks

Wide locks

A narrow lock usually has a single gate on the uphill side and mitered double gates at the lower end. Locks that can accommodate two narrowboats side-by-side generally have double gates at either end. Some of the Thames locks can handle any number of watercraft. The etiquette chapter has more about wide locks.

Flight of locks

A flight of locks is simply a series of locks that are treated as a group. Each lock will be in sight of the next and the boat crew probably will not re-board the boat after operating the lock, choosing instead to walk to the next lock to prepare it. Often a large flight has additional water storage and pumping facilities. The Tardebigge flight of 30 locks on the Worcester & Birmingham Canal has a nearby reservoir to provide enough water. The Caen Hill flight of 16 locks has an extra offset pound between each set of locks.

A flight of locks is handled pretty much the same way as a single lock, but it can take all day to get through them all. It's a good idea to schedule a flight first thing in the morning.

Staircase locks

Staircase locks share gates—the downhill gate of one lock is the uphill gate of the next. The Foxton Locks on the Leicester Line of the Grand Union Canal are two sets of five staircase locks, with expanded pounds to supply water.

Foxton Locks
goo.gl/OLQg2W

There is usually a lock-keeper at a larger staircase lock, ensuring that for boats going downhill, only the topmost lock is full and the others are empty, or for boats going uphill, that all the locks are full except for the bottom-most lock. If you try to pour water into a lock that's already full, it will overflow the gates and the chamber walls.

Generally staircase locks are negotiated much faster than a similar number of lock flights, however you may have to wait in line longer

A staircase is negotiated quite differently than a flight of locks. All the locks in a staircase must be turned in the favor of a boat (or boats) going uphill or downhill. On single locks, uphill and downhill boats take turns going through the locks, but a staircase lockkeeper might have several boats pass through the lock in the same direction.

I've read posts online suggesting how important it is to contact the lockkeeper when you arrive at a staffed staircase lock. And a lockkeeper can be quite comfortable in a cozy cottage. He might not come out to you; you may have to knock on the door. Whatever you do, don't go through the lock on your own. A boater headed down against three boats coming up will receive a tongue lashing from the lockkeeper they won't soon forget.

When a crew approaches a staircase lock, many of the usual rules apply. If the nearest gate is open, that's a pretty good sign the boat can proceed, but the lookouts need to scan the entire staircase to make sure there isn't already a boat in one of the chambers headed in the opposite direction.

Going Downhill

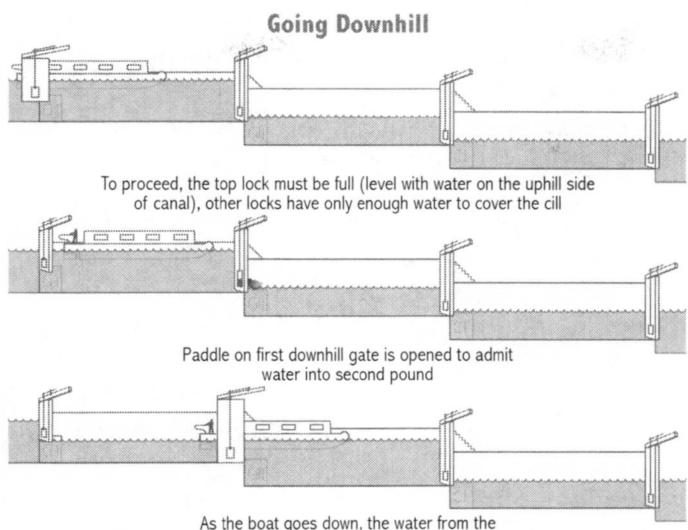

To proceed, the top lock must be full (level with water on the uphill side of canal), other locks have only enough water to cover the cill

Paddle on first downhill gate is opened to admit water into second pound

As the boat goes down, the water from the previous lock is drained into the next lock

Going Uphill

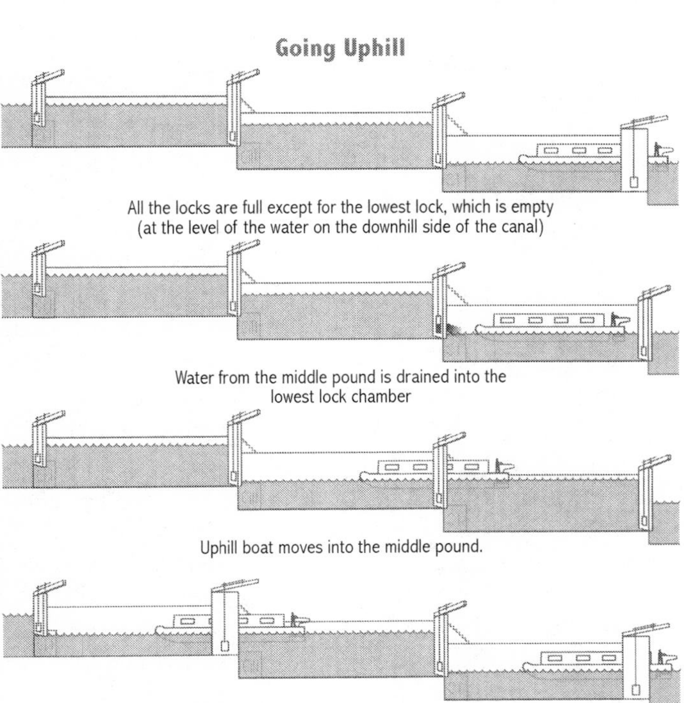

All the locks are full except for the lowest lock, which is empty (at the level of the water on the downhill side of the canal)

Water from the middle pound is drained into the lowest lock chamber

Uphill boat moves into the middle pound.

Another boat going in the same direction can use the water held in higher pounds

Going downhill, all the chambers except the topmost must be empty. However the "empty" locks should not be completely empty or there might not be enough water to float over the cill between each lock. Going uphill, all the steps except the bottommost should be full.

Unfortunately there's always a chance on a longer staircase that you might run out of water. Because gates don't meet perfectly there's always some leakage—that full chamber of water on the top step might not be a full chamber's worth by the fourth step, so a boat crew might have to let more water into the top step and then bring it down to the fourth step—but not too much water or again you might overflow the chamber on the fourth step.

Longer staircases, however, are often set up differently. There are overflow channels to prevent flooding the chamber and holding pounds of extra water to make up a chamber that's too shallow. You should check with the lockkeeper or read any posted instructions on how to operate such locks.

Guillotine locks
They're not as frightening as they sound. Instead of the gate swinging out, the gate moves up and down like a camera shutter. Sometimes they are electrically operated. Like all paddles, open them slowly at first.

Running out of water

Occasionally canals run low on water and sometimes they actually run out of water. Often you can correct the first problem but not the second.

Running low on water is a problem that usually presents itself when moving a boat uphill through a lock. Here's the scenario: after entering the lock from the downhill gates you close the lower gates and open the uphill paddles to allow water into the lock chamber. After the water in the chamber equalizes with the water in the uphill pound, you open the uphill gates and attempt to drive your boat out of the lock.

Canals run out of water for a variety of reasons, including: low rainfall; evaporation; leaks in the canal bed; leaking canal gates; increased traffic on the canal; leaving paddles and gates open accidentally or intentionally; and canal and aqueduct breaches

Then you hear a horrendous shrieking noise and realize the boat is not moving. You've caught your boat on the cill (*read the explanation on the next page*) because there wasn't quite enough water in the pound to raise the water level in the lock chamber sufficiently.

Remember the pound is the water between locks. If locks are closely spaced, then the amount of water is small. If the next uphill lock is ten miles away, it's enormous.

What to do

Your best option is to find a lockkeeper, which is easiest to do during the height of the boating season on a busy stretch of canal. Out of season somewhere on a long flight of locks, you may be out of luck.

You should keep handy the phone number of your boat hire and the local office of the relevant navigation authority. And it wouldn't hurt to direct message that local office via twitter.

If you can't find a lockkeeper, you'll need to send a member of the crew to empty the nearest uphill lock, which may release enough water to float your boat over the cill. Of course you may have to do this repeatedly as your progress uphill from lock to lock. If the next lock is miles distant, however, you may be out of luck.

Catastrophic water loss

Occasionally a canal catastrophically loses water from a canal bank breach or vandals leaving paddles open at one or more locks. There's little you can do about this other than call someone to report the situation and to put the kettle on.

Lock gates are mostly built of oak. The paddles used to be made of elm, but Dutch elm disease has made elm scarce and so now paddles are also made of oak.

Danger

As mentioned before, locks are relatively simple and you'll soon become an expert at turning them, but with skill often comes complacency. Please be sober when turning a lock, especially the driver. Carelessness can cause damage to the boat, damage to the lock, usually damage to both and very, very infrequently loss of life.

In an abundance of caution, some boat hires advise not to step on the gunwales or roof of a boat, ignoring that the gangplank, center line and poles are stored on the roof and may be otherwise inaccessible.

Beware the cill

The biggest danger is being caught on the cill. The cill is the masonry or concrete structure against which the uphill gate closes. There's a similar ledge against which the downhill gate closes, but it's less noticeable. Staircase locks, however, share cills. Some cills are stair-stepped, so you might think you've cleared it but you haven't.

You're at most risk going downhill, when the stern of the boat is closest to the cill. It's difficult to get the front of the boat caught on the cill going uphill, but it is possible to swamp the front of the boat when opening the uphill paddles too quickly. It's a good idea to close the front doors of the boat when going uphill and to open uphill paddles gradually. If there are both ground and gate paddles on the uphill side, open the ground paddles first until the boat is high enough that the inflow from the gate paddles won't swamp the boat.

Rebound

The other danger is rebound, caused by the flow of water into the lock chamber from the uphill sluice or gate paddles. Going uphill, you might have taken care to avoid the uphill gate, probably applying a little reverse thrust to keep the boat from actually hitting the gate. But as

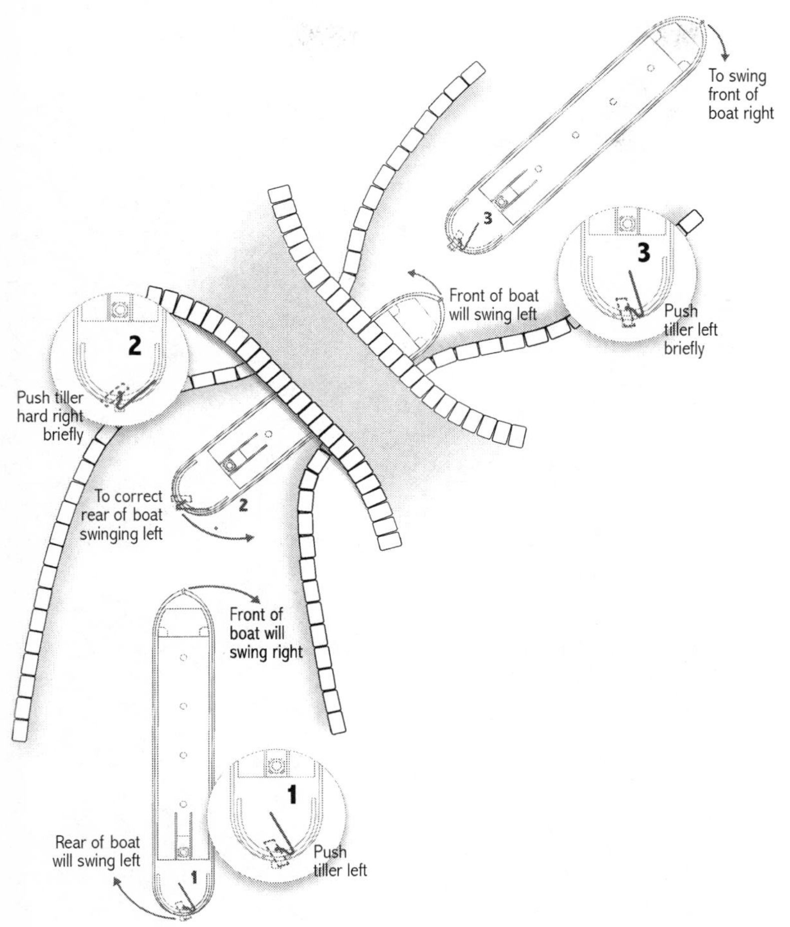

water comes into the chamber, it hits the closed lower gate, rebounds and pushes the boat forward.

Falling in

Throw a life preserver to anyone who falls into the lock chamber and if possible a line. Put the engine into neutral and try to keep the boat still. Close all paddles, however it may be necessary to either let water in if the chamber is almost full to allow the person to swim to the edge of the chamber and climb out. Or release water

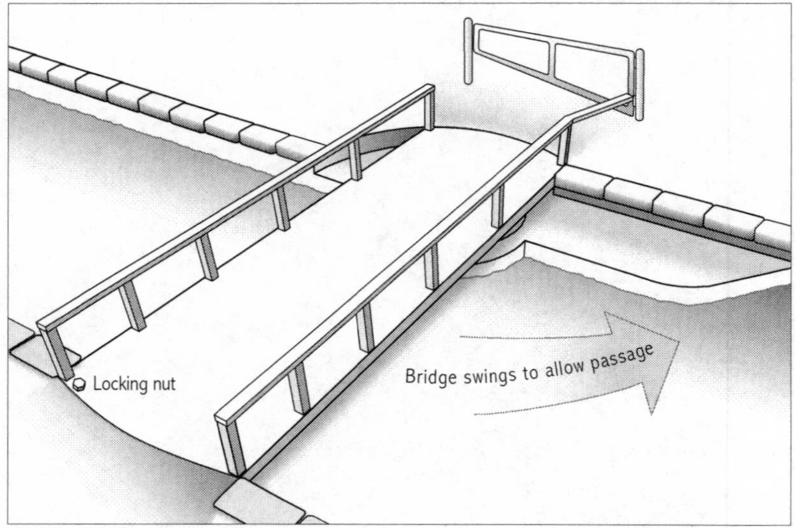

A swing bridge

from the chamber if it is almost empty and open the lower gate. Don't jump in to save them; you'll just end up with two people in the lock.

Going too fast

Going too fast through a lock is probably what causes the most cumulative damage to a lock. The gates last about 20 years before replacing. You'll notice they're protected with steel plates, but careless and drunken boaters have occasionally broken out the vertical slats or even dislodged gates.

Open both lock gates when entering or leaving a lock. Don't push open a partially closed gate with the boat's hull—that could damage the edge of the gate and cause it to leak.

Bridges

Navigating a bog-standard bridge is not too difficult, as long as you recall the advice given in the how to steer chapter. You'll need to remember that when you make

An hydraulically operated lift bridge

the front of the boat turn right, the rear of the boat will turn left. Which means that you'll need to correct the drift of the rear of the boat as you go under the arch of the bridge, because invariably the canal bends either before, after, or before and after the bridge.

Swing bridges

Swing bridges are treated similar to locks. They'll be a spot to moor on the other side of the bridge where a boat can pull aside to let someone off who will swing the bridge open.

At the least, there will be some sort of locking nut or chain that needs to be removed with a wrench, but some swing bridges may be locked, requiring a CRT key or handcuff key. In addition, there may be crossing guards that need to be put in place to prevent traffic or pedestrians from driving through the turned bridge.

Swing bridges are easy to turn—so easy in fact that you could accidentally slam them against the wooden or stone stops. You should slow the bridge as it reaches the end of its travel.

Lift bridges

Again, treat lift bridges like locks. You'll need to send someone ahead to lift the bridge. Some bridges are raised and lowered by a rope (you may need someone tall enough and heavy enough to move the bridge or wear a loaded backpack for extra weight), some have a hydraulic crank (it's a bit tedious but effective) and some are operated electrically.

It's important to fully raise a lift bridge before driving your boat through because the clearance is often minimal.

You may occasionally find lift and swing bridges that require an operator and you may need to call ahead to arrange a meeting. The Canal & River Trust has experimented with bridges on the Gloucester & Sharpness Canal operated with a phone app, but it's only available to licensed boat owners.

The Standedge Tunnel on the Huddersfield Narrow Canal is both the highest, longest (3.25 miles) and deepest canal tunnel in Britain. It is one of the Seven Wonders of the Waterways. You need to arrange passage through the tunnel three days in advance.

Tunnels

Standedge Tunnel
goo.gl/SNØzDw

Even if you're not claustrophobic, canal tunnels are intimidating if you stop to consider the enormous weight resting on bricks laid two hundred years ago, if you stop to worry about the possibility of meeting a boat coming the other direction in the tunnel and if you worry about your engine dying halfway through.

Some tunnels have requirements/specifications boaters must adhere to or have signaling that controls traffic through the tunnel.

In general, you should ensure before entering a tunnel:

- Everyone not remaining within the cabin of the boat is wearing a life vest.
- That there are no oncoming boats already in the tunnel
- That the headlamp is lit
- That the driver has a torch/flashlight
- That all exposed flames are extinguished
- That some interior lighting is turned on
- That the horn has been sounded for at least two seconds
- That children and pets are safe
- That no one is doing anything stupid (sitting on the roof of the boat, dangling a leg over the side)

When possible, try to share the tunnel with other boats going the same direction.

After entering the tunnel:

- Don't tailgate
- Don't blind the driver with flash photography (happened to me)

This is the old toll house at Kings Norton Junction, where the Worcester & Birmingham and Stratford-upon-Avon canals meet

Apparently some people have trouble keeping course, but I've never had that problem. The advice is to look at only one side of the tunnel instead of looking into the gloom ahead. Some tunnels curve as well.

A 2014 tragic accident in the Harecastle Tunnel has prompted the Canal & River Trust to recommend everyone not remaining within the main cabin to wear a life vest. Unfortunately someone at the tiller of a boat was knocked overboard by the very low ceiling of the tunnel and drowned.

You might want to wear a hat and rain gear when going through a tunnel as well as a life vest if you're standing at the tiller. Tunnel ceilings can drip a surprising amount of water.

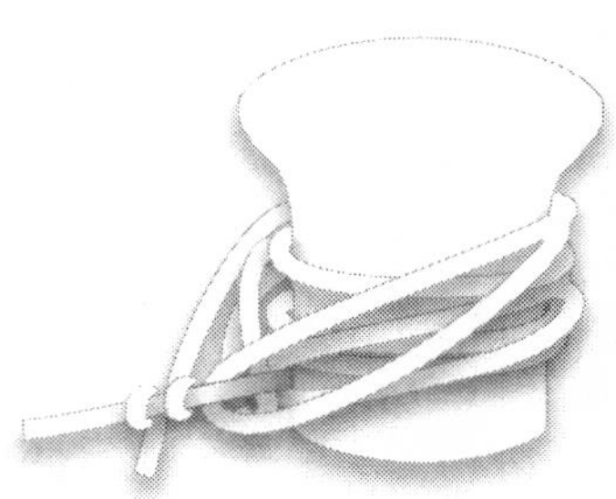

Knots and ropes

Tying up the boat is an everyday narrowboat task that many people find challenging. I consider myself a capable person with a good grasp of mechanics. I've rebuilt a car engine and a carburetor and I build furniture, but I can't tie a knot to save my life. The excellent *Boaters Handbook* has a page that shows common knots, but static diagrams are extremely difficult to follow.

Do yourself a favor and take some time to work out any knots in the front, stern or center lines of your boat. Lines on hire boats always have knots left over from previous boaters. These knots can get in the way when you're holding a boat against a lock or trying to moor.

Animated Knots by Grog
goo.gl/cgYZtZ

The solution is to visit the website Animated Knots by Grog. There is no better way to learn how to tie knots, as the process is demonstrated either as step-by-step animations or can be viewed on YouTube with narration. (In fairness, there are several good knot websites.) You can even download an iOS or Android app. Knots are divided into sections: basic, boating, climbing, fishing, etc, and even better, the description for each knot lists uses, cautions and alternatives.

Knots for the Cut
goo.gl/BWP5B8

If you don't have Internet access or you dropped your iPad in the canal, however, you can still refer to the drawings in this book. They're based on the drawings from the *Boaters Handbook*, but much expanded. The Inland Waterways Association also sells *Knots for the Cut* by Ben Selfe.

Canalman's hitch: bollard, spike

The single most useful knot is the canalman's or lighterman's hitch (a lighter is a flat-bottomed barge), which isn't actually a knot, and that's its chief advantage. It's very secure if done correctly but it's also very easy to remove. This hitch is most suited for use on bollards, either on the towpath or brought back to the bitts (they look like mini-bollards) on the stern of the boat. It's actually quite easy to tie, although it's not so easy to follow these diagrams. Definitely visit the website mentioned earlier or search YouTube for other videos about this hitch.

Step 1
Loop a line around a bollard twice (called a round turn).

Step 2
Pass a bight (loop) of rope *underneath* the line from the boat and then draw the bight over the top of the bollard.

Step 3, 4
Take the end of the line and wrap another loop over the bollard *in the same direction as the original loops*. This will require you to cross over the line from the boat.

Canalman's or lighterman's hitch

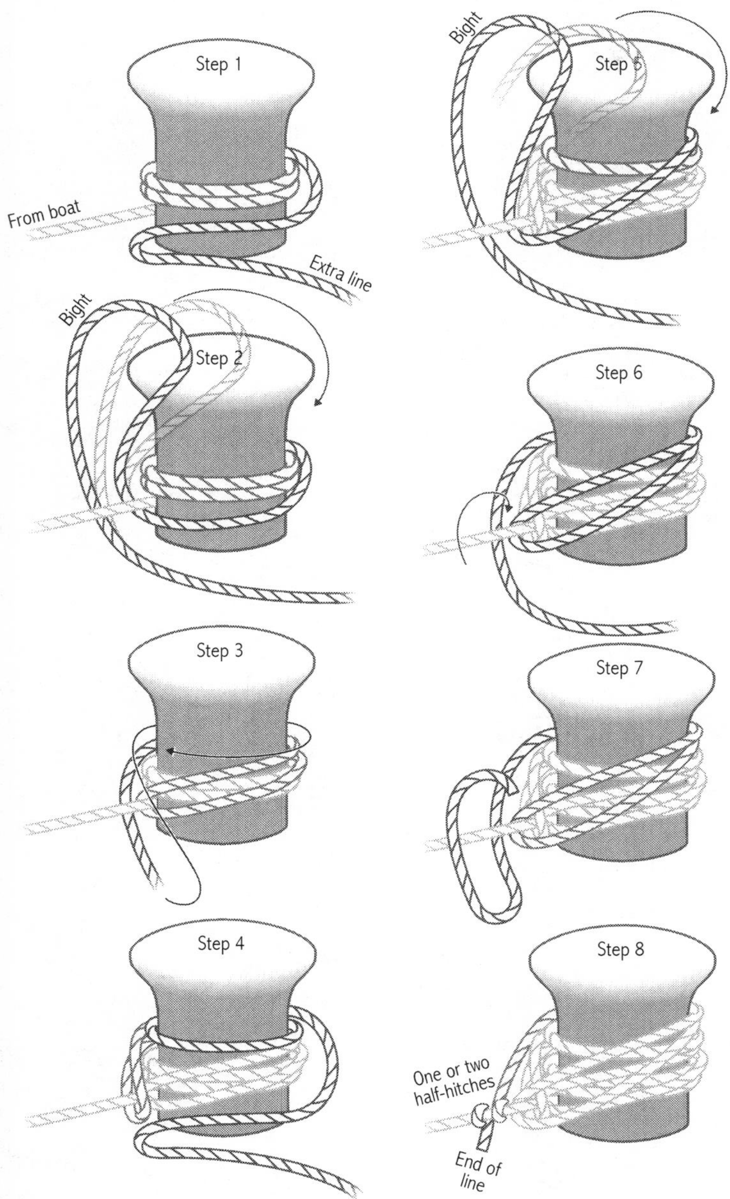

Step 5
Then pass another bight underneath the line from the boat and again draw it over the bollard, just like you did in Step 2.

Step 6–8
The remaining steps are optional. You can pass the end of the line back through the opening indicated by the arrow to make a half hitch. Add another half hitch for safety or to use up rope. If you have a lot a lot of leftover line, you could make the half hitches with a bight of rope.

Half-hitch

Bowline: mooring pin, ring

The canalman's hitch works best on a bollard. If you're attaching a line from the boat to a mooring ring or mooring spike with an eye hole, the bowline (pronounced BO-lin) knot is preferred. It won't slip and

Bowline

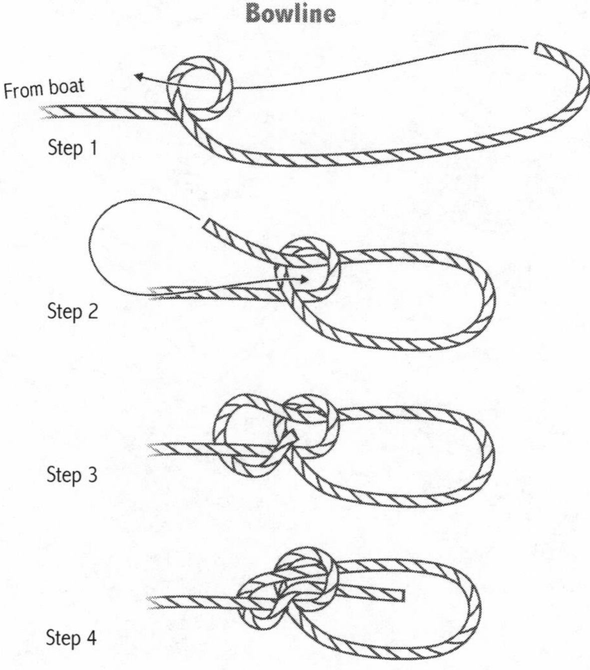

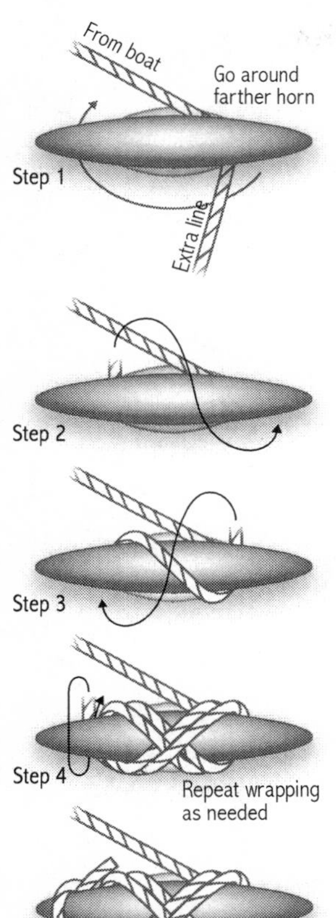

can be easily untied if there is no load on the line.

Step 1
Make a loop and pass the end of the line through it.

Step 2, 3
Pass the end of the line around the back of the line from the boat

Step 4
Pass the back of the line back through the loop you created in step 1.

Cleat hitch: cleat

The front line is probably already tied to a cleat on the prow of the boat and you'll run that line through a mooring ring on the towpath and then back to the boat, wrapping it around the same cleat.

Step 1
Wrap the line from the boat around the base of the cleat. In the example, you see the line first wraps clockwise because the line is coming from the left. Always wrap around the farther horn first.

Step 2, 3
The line wraps clockwise to the left horn and then up and over and crosses back to the right horn. Then the line goes back underneath the right horn and up and over and crosses back to the left horn.

Step 4
Repeat this figure eight pattern as many times as pos-

sible. If you don't have enough line to cross at least twice (as shown), then considering tying directly to the mooring ring on the towpath.

Step 5
Secure the line by either going under a horn and trapping it under itself or tying the loose end with a half hitch to the line from the boat.

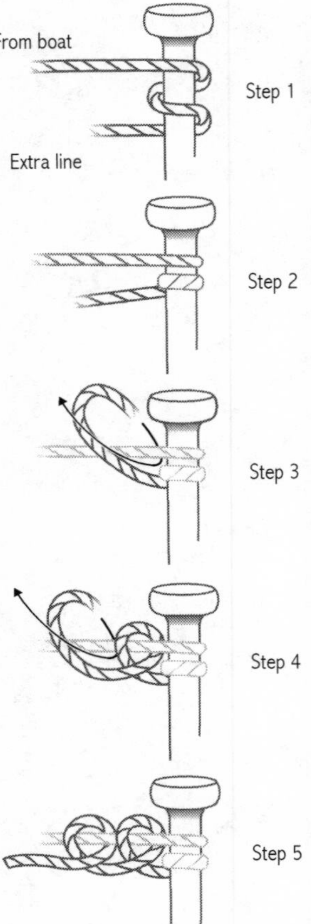

Round turn with two half hitches: bollard, mooring pin

The round turn with two half hitches hardly looks like a knot that can be relied on to secure a boat, but it does work and can be tied with one hand, the other hand taking up the strain (keeping the boat close). You can add additional turns in windy weather or if there is heavy traffic.

Step 1
The two round turns go around the mooring spike. Add more turns as necessary.

Step 2
Tighten the turns.

Step 3, 4
Pass the end of the line over the line from the boat and then through the opening to make a half hitch.

Step 5
Add another half hitch. Two half hitches add up to a clove hitch, which by itself could slip, but not with the round turn. If you have a lot of extra line, you can make the two half hitches with a bight (a loop of line). A clove

How to coil a mooring line

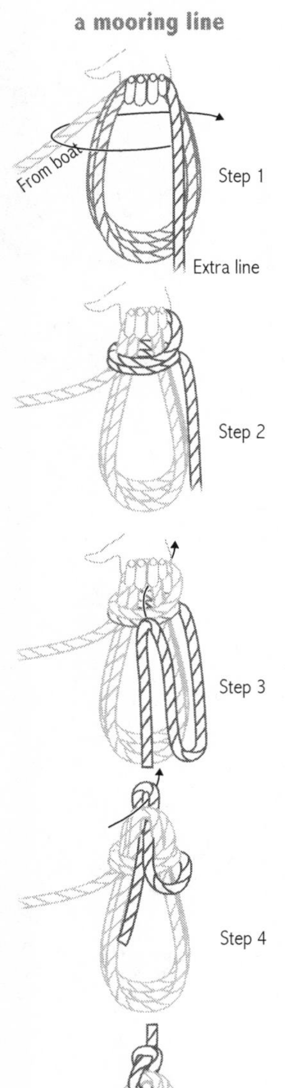

hitch made with a bight makes for a quick release.

Stow your lines carefully

You'll want to keep your lines neat and in order. A good place to stow the end of the center line is in the life ring just forward of the rear hatch. The front line is usually easy to stow in the front well, tucked into a corner where you can't trip over it. It's the stern line that is the hardest to stow and also the most important to stow safely because a trailing stern line can be caught up by the propeller.

Step 1
Probably the easiest way to coil your line is to hold a few equal length loops in your hand. Slightly roll the line with each loop to prevent twisting.

Step 2
Wrap one or more loops around all the loops, just below your hand.

Step 3, 4
Next you're going to pull a bight through the opening just below your hand and above the wraps you applied in step 2.

Step 5
To finish, pull the end of the line (the bitter end) through the loop of the bight. On a cruiser stern boat, you can hang the coiled line from the railing, using a clove hitch, explained below.

Clove hitch: railing

A clove hitch is not very secure and can easily loosen, but it has many uses because it can be so easily removed. You wouldn't use it to moor your boat, but the clove hitch is perfect for hanging that coiled rope or a fender.

Be aware of where your lines are. Don't place your foot in a loop because it will become a noose when taut. Don't let your fingers or hand be trapped between the rope and a bollard, spike or ring.

Be especially careful of your lines when underway. We encountered a couple that had let their stern line dangle. When they put the throttle in reverse, it sucked in the line and tangled it around the propeller. Luckily they were able to open the weed hatch and free the line.

Step 1

Loop your line over a railing or post. The clove hitch is most secure over a round rail or post. On the underside, pass the end of the line over the line from the coil.

Step 2

Loop your line over the railing again.

Step 3

To finish, pass the end of the line underneath the second loop you made in step 2 and pull the end up.

Step 4

If you have extra line, you can pass a bight through the second loop in step 3, making a quick release.

Fenders

Your boat is probably equipped with fenders (just a hard rubber tube with a rope running through it) that you can hang off the side of your boat when moored against a towpath lined with stone, wood or corrugated metal. You won't need them against a grassy bank.

There's usually some sort of railing that runs along the roof of the boat where you can tie off a fender. Hang it at a height that puts it between the towpath lining and the edge of the boat, otherwise during the night, you'll hear the boat banging against the stone.

Most people pull up the fenders when the boat is moving and definitely in a lock (so they don't get caught in any lock mechanisms), although they can be useful when sharing a lock with another boat.

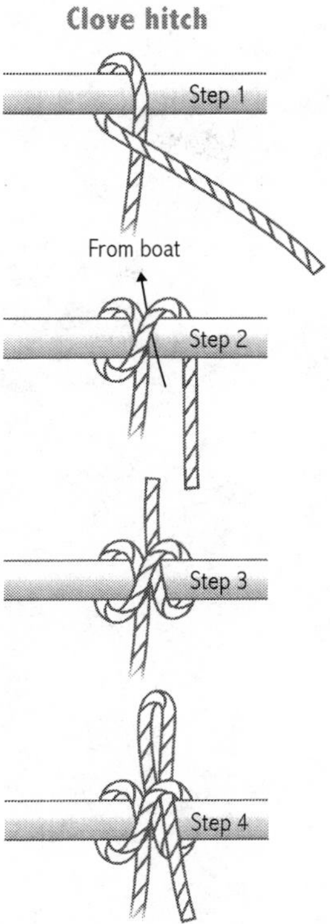

Looking toward the rear of the boat. Note the clothes hanging under the curtains on the right and the towels hanging on the left. They're hanging from the rail that's there to keep the curtains against the walls.

Etiquette / waterway rules

Most of the etiquette and rules you need to observe on the waterway are common sense, but sometimes it can be hard to remember the rationale for some of them.

Passing

- Pass oncoming boats on the right (even though you drive a car on the left in the UK)
- Reduce speed when passing a moving boat
- When approaching bridges, the closer boat should go first, but on rivers, the boat going downstream has the right of way
- Don't try to overtake another boat unless the other boat has clearly reduced speed, moved aside and indicated to you that you may pass
- Larger boats, dredges and commercial boats have the right of way and can tell you what side to pass on

Underway

- Don't leave a wake that reaches the canal bank
- Pass moored boats as slowly as possible
- Don't tailgate other boats

Learn the horn signals

OK, realistically you'll be the only one on the canal who understands them, but it can still be useful to know the horn signals (the button will be very near the tiller). Actually, you're unlikely to hear these signals on a canal—they're more common on rivers when you will meet commercial boats. If you hear another boat sound these signals, it means that boat will:

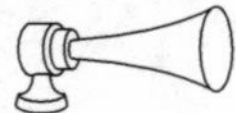

- One blast: Going to the right
- Two blasts: Going to the left
- Three blasts: Slow down, stop or go backwards
- Four blasts–pause–one blast: Turning around to the right
- Four blasts–pause–two blasts: Turning around to the left

All boats should sound one long blast (at least two seconds) when approaching a blind bend or before entering a tunnel.

Lights

Commercial and larger boats often have white running lights fore and aft and green, starboard (right-hand) and red, port (left-hand) navigation lights. If at night you see the red light on the right side, the boat is headed toward you.

Locks

- If sharing a lock, the larger boat enters first
- For single locks, with boats approaching in both directions, the boat with the lock already turned in its favor goes first
- Don't dawdle if there are other boats behind you
- Don't rush other boat crews turning the lock

Mooring

- Don't cross the towpath with your mooring lines
- Mark your mooring pins with a carrier bag or something reflec-

tive or very light colored. If it is a plastic bag make sure it won't just catch the wind and sail away!

- You should share a mooring ring or bollard with another boat, but don't entangle your mooring lines with theirs
- Don't moor near water points, bridges, locks, blind bends, weirs or anywhere that doing so would be a nuisance
- Moor only on the towpath side unless otherwise indicated

Canal life

- Don't pee in the water
- Don't dump sewage or hazardous materials in the water
- Don't feed the ducks bread. It ultimately isn't good for them and uneaten bread fosters algae. If you must feed them, better to give them oats, corn or defrosted frozen peas. In general, don't feed the wildlife.
- Don't swim in the canals. It's icky (see don't pee in the water).

Observe silence

Enjoy the quiet of the waterways, especially at night when moored. Avoid running the engine at night. Shouting to be heard rarely works. Some moorings are specifically marked as quiet zones.

You see the same people again and again as you travel the canal if you're going in the same direction. If you get into an argument at one lock, you'll just end up resuming it at the next one. Better to avoid getting into an argument before it turns into an argy-bargy.

On the boat

I've been very fortunate to sail with my husband, my best friend and her brother. We get along pretty well, which doesn't mean we don't have the occasional disagreement, but being reasonable adults we get over it. We're all of the same temperaments and we have similar enough interests that we can usually agree on what to do next.

We generally take turns driving the boat, turning the locks, tying up the boat, etc, but we all have things we're better at and tasks get apportioned appropriately. We are comically disorganized when it comes to buying groceries for the trip and we're all unsure enough what we're doing that we dither, but despite all that, we make a pretty good crew.

My friend Lee wanted me to mention how extraordinarily kind, polite, helpful and friendly the British people have been to us on our trips. They seem to delight in the idea of Americans finding their canals so interesting. Whenever we sit next to someone at a pub or on a train, we're asked where we're from, how long we're staying and told not to miss some attraction or to stop at this pub or restaurant. The British people are definitely not standoffish.

Politeness is our greatest virtue. If someone makes a cup of tea, he or she asks if the driver would like a cuppa. If someone plans to take a shower, that person asks if anyone needs to use the bathroom first. There are other fundamental rules to follow like knock first before entering the bathroom. I have yet to be on a boat where the bathroom door locks easily or properly.

I hope our crew gets to do another narrowboat vacation very soon, and this time I won't hog the tiller.

Checklist

While planning

- ☐ Book boat as early as possible to save money
- ☐ Check for planned waterway closures
- ☐ Find out any restrictions, requirements for travel on your planned waterway
- ☐ If planning an urban waterway (like Regent's Canal in London), check for other planned transportation closures, like work on the Underground
- ☐ Check tourism websites to see what events are scheduled along your waterway
- ☐ Check opening/closing times for museums, stately homes, etc, you plan to visit
- ☐ Plan how to recharge electronic devices
- ☐ Download digital maps along your proposed route
- ☐ Make sure you know the PIN numbers of all your debit/credit cards
- ☐ Renew passport if necessary
- ☐ Create a list of what you'll need while on the boat, including a grocery list
- ☐ Read the boater's handbook provided by your waterway authority

Just before leaving

- ☐ Tell your cellular provider you'll be out of the country and find a suitable international data and voice plan to avoid roaming charges
- ☐ Notify credit card companies that you'll be out of the country
- ☐ Update downloaded digital maps (Google maps need to be updated every 30 days; see "Google Maps" on page 122)
- ☐ Download/print out a guide for your waterway (See "guides for individual canals" on page 117). Downloaded CRT guides are updated with current information.
- ☐ Check for last-minute closures
- ☐ Contact authorities if necessary to register, get permissions for your planned waterway

After arriving

- ☐ If possible, visit your waterway before boarding your boat; especially watch other boaters turning a lock if you're new
- ☐ Check for any un-planned waterway closures. A boater might have damaged a lock and it would make more sense to travel in the other direction on the canal. Contact your boat hire to see what they suggest.
- ☐ Contact authorities if necessary to register, get permissions for your planned waterway (some canals can only be booked the day before)

Resources

Organizations

Canal & River Trust (CRT)
The Canal & River Trust Ⓦ is a charitable organization that owns and manages 2,000 miles of waterways in England and Wales (where it's called Glandwr Cymru). The trust is the successor to British Waterways, the quasi-governmental organization that previously owned and managed the waterways (you can still see BW signs along the canals). The trust received the assets of British Waterways (and presumably the debts), with the intent that as a charitable organization, it could better manage government grants, donations and help from volunteers. Most but not all of the still navigable canals in England and Wales are administered by the CRT.

The CRT website is an invaluable aid to boaters, from the boater's handbook to the stoppages page to the guides for individual canals Ⓦ. The latter is very useful because it will be compiled as an up-to-date lock-by-lock, bridge-by-bridge guide. Remember to **generate a guide immediately before your trip.** You can also watch The Boater's Handbook as a video Ⓦ at YouTube.

Stream advisories

If you plan to travel rivers, find out local stream advisories Ⓦ, such as those provided by the Environment Agency. The Environment Agency Ⓦ is responsible for many of the waterways not maintained by the CRT. There are efforts ongoing to move control of some Anglian waterways from the EA to the CRT.

Scottish Canals

The five canals in Scotland (only four of which are still navigable) were also part of British Waterways, but when the Canal & River Trust was created, the Scottish government decided to retain ownership of those canals and created Scottish Canals Ⓦ. You can also download skipper's guides and read about stoppages or other notices Ⓦ at the website.

Waterways Ireland

Waterways Ireland Ⓦ is the "implementation body" responsible for the canals in Northern Ireland and the Republic of Ireland, as created in the 1999 Belfast Agreement.

IWAI

The Inland Waterways Association of Ireland Ⓦ is a volunteer organization that will also prove invaluable, with online charts of the waterways and numerous books, guides and maps Ⓦ to buy. By joining the organization, you'll also receive their quarterly publication *Inland Waterways News.*

IWA

The Inland Waterways Association Ⓦ is a UK-wide charity that works with (and sometimes argues against) the Canal & River Trust and other navigation authorities. See *"Recovery" on page 20* for more information. One of the great benefits of joining the IWA is to receive the *Waterways* magazine, as well as discounts on boat hires, pubs and other services.

Publications

Narrowboat, the Inland Waterways Heritage Magazine, offers an historical look at the canals. A sample issue is available through the website and back issues can be read online. It is the perfect magazine for a beginning gongoozler.

Towpath Talk and *Tillergraph* are free waterway-related newspapers that you can find at marinas, tourist bureaus or canal trust visitor centers, or you can subscribe to have it delivered or you can read it free online.

Waterways World is another print magazine that can also be read online with a subscription. These publications are geared for liveaboards, but the news stories will help anyone planning a canal trip.

Training

Realistically most people can learn to handle a narrowboat and turn locks pretty quickly, but it's understandable that some people want specific instruction beyond the cursory training the boat hire offers. The Royal Yachting Association offers several two-day courses that would be appropriate for narrowboaters and you would have the prestige of displaying your RYA diploma at home (smoking jacket not required). You can also buy the RYA International Certificate of Competence Handbook for further study, although the ICC is not required to operate a narrowboat. You can also find training just by searching for "narrowboat training" and adding the name of the waterway you'll be traveling.

Websites

There are many, many websites devoted to narrowboating. I've found invaluable information at Canal Junction, Narrowboat World, Pennine Waterways and the

Narrowboat Users Group on facebook. Canalworld.net is an online forum. Much of the emphasis on these websites is for liveaboards, but there's still a lot of information US boaters will appreciate. They also offer a glimpse into the kind of community we can only experience vicariously.

Met Office

Find sunny days for your trip at the Met Office, the national weather service for the UK.

YouTube

There's a lot available on YouTube about narrowboating, but I don't want to post any URLs, because the more popular a video is, the more likely the television channel that produced it will want it removed. Search for *Great Canal Journeys*, presented by Prunella (Sybil from *Fawlty Towers*) Scales and Jeremy West, *Barging Round Britain* with John Sergeant and *Canal Walks* with Julia Bradbury.

I can, however, give you URLs for Cruising the Cut, The Narrowboat Experience, Journey with Jono and London Boat Girl.

The various canal trusts also have their own YouTube channels, including the Canal & River Trust and Scottish Canals.

Individual canal trusts

There are a host of trusts, friends of and societies for individual canals and some have their own publications, guides, websites, museums and facebook pages. The Canal Junction website has a list of these groups, but with so many, not every link is necessarily up to date.

If you plan to travel a canal, search for groups associated with the canal. Searching for "Kennet and Avon friends of" will return a link to the Kennet and Avon Canal Trust, for instance. Searching for "UK canal trust" should also return a very long list of trusts.

Museums

There are many museums in the UK that address the history of the canals, such as the London Canal Museum at King's Cross; the museums of the Canal & River Trust, including the National Waterways Museums in Cheshire or in Gloucester and the Stoke Bruerne Canal Museum; and the K&A Canal Trust Museum Ⓦ in Devizes.

Again, search for your canal plus museum. Searching for "Trent Mersey Canal museum" returns a link to the Etruria Industrial Museum Ⓦ. Josiah Wedgwood created his Etruria Works in Staffordshire and Jesse Shirley's steam-powered bone and flint mills supplied manufacturers like Wedgwood with raw materials. The museum, which is next to the Caldon Canal (a branch of the Trent and Mersey), operates Shirley's steam engine on certain weekends.

There are probably numerous historic pumping stations, boat lifts, mills and boat yards along any canal you plan to visit.

Books/guides/maps

Your single most invaluable resource for many canals is a *Pearson's Canal Companion* Ⓦ. These small booklets are a travelogue for your journey with a clear opinion of what others would consider progress ("Tesco have breezed into town, but personally we will still beat a path to Vermeulen's delicatessen …"). The maps indicate towpath quality, laundries, moorings (private, prohibited, public), bridges, fish and chip shops, post offices, winding holes, locks, water points, showers, pump outs and much more. You'll have descriptions of towns and restaurants that are a little arch, like "Bray: Smug gastronomic cornucopia famous for its

17th Century vicar and his weathercock attitude to politics and religion."

Despite the attitude (or perhaps because of it), you'll enjoy the companion, although the maps can take a bit of getting used to. They don't necessarily progress in the direction you're traveling and each map is usually positioned to the landscape orientation of the book, meaning north is rarely up. The *Pearson's* guides are available on Amazon.

Another resource is the *Collins/Nicholson Waterways Guides* and *Waterways Map* of Great Britain. These are closer to actual maps and you can find them on Amazon. They make a good companion to the *Pearson's Canal Companion*.

Our canal library also includes *Our Great Canal Journeys* by Timothy West, LTC Rolt's *Narrow Boat* and *Great Waterways Journeys* by Derek Pratt.

Maps

I've created a number of Google maps for UK waterways, generally based on information obtained from the relevant navigational authority. They can be copied for your own use.

The maps generated by the Canal & River Trust are also good companions as they generally run west to east with north up. Another option would be to order the Ordnance Survey maps appropriate to your canal. You can even order a custom map centered on any location you desire.

If you would like your maps available on your mobile

device for offline use, you can download a map of your canal, or at least 120,000-square kilometer chunks of it, using the Google Maps iOS or Android app.

Of course while connected to the Internet, you can also walk down the towpaths of some canals using street view on Google Maps. The Llangollen; Kennet & Avon; Liverpool and Leeds; and Regent's canals all have some street view portions. By walking along the canals in street view, you can see precisely what type of mooring is available, whether the towpath is suitable for cycling and just how far that pub really is. More street views of canals are being added. Another Google map-based website that's useful is OpenSignal.com, which shows the cellular signal strength in the area you're traveling.

Open Canal Map is available as an Android app or as a map that can be opened using the Google Maps app on a phone or tablet or even with a web browser on a phone or tablet. It lists every canal in far more detail than my own maps, but it can take some time to load and is a little cumbersome to navigate.

CanalPlanAC is a website that helps you plan a trip. You can enter a waterway or a starting point or destination and obtain an appropriate route tailored to your how many hours per day you wish to travel. The website also has searchable database of individual locations, with information about mooring and services, photographs and maps.

Tourist guides

We've had some amazing coincidences while on our narrowboat trips, such as town festivals and open houses that fall on the day that we're in a town, but we've also missed some opportunities by a day. No trip can be perfect no matter how carefully it's planned, but it's good to know in advance what trade-offs you'll have to make.

To really take advantage of those opportunities, you should visit the website of the various tourism agencies promoting the cities and towns along your canal. Some of them are quite obvious, such as VisitLondon.com, the official visitor guide. But smaller cities, towns and villages also have their own tourism websites. For instance, there is a website just for the Falkirk Wheel, but if you search for "visit Falkirk," you'll also find the website VisitFalkirk.com for the city of Falkirk and the surrounding area. One of the useful items you'll discover at the website is TheLoop, a bus service that stops at the two Falkirk train stations, the Wheel and The Kelpies—30-meter high horse head statues along the Forth & Clyde Canal that many associate with the Wheel, but are not actually at the Wheel.

Other city and local tourism websites include VisitLiverpool.com and VisitBirmingham.com. Of course there are also websites for the whole of Britain and for each of the kingdoms: VisitEngland.com, VisitWales.com and VisitScotland.com. There's also DiscoverNorthernIreland.com and DiscoverIreland.ie.

These official tourism websites have calendars of events and usually a lodging database: put in the city where you wish to stay and the dates and you'll see a listing of hotels, serviced apartments and bed and breakfasts sorted by price and ratings.

Transportation

Many of the places where you pick up a boat are in relatively remote places, not necessarily accessible by train, my preferred way to travel in the UK.

Trains

For those old enough to remember, the four big British rail companies were nationalized in 1965 to become British Rail with its familiar double-arrow logo, but in 1996, British Rail was privatized and became National Rail (with pretty much the same logo). The National Rail website can be used to book train travel anywhere in the UK, or you can book through the actual train operator, such as ScotRail or South West Trains.

Things to remember about train travel:

- Keep your ticket handy, a conductor will come by to check. I always forget the safe place I put it.
- Regional trains and inter-city trains almost always have a coach with a restroom
- Regional trains and inter-city trains almost always have a buffet car or someone pushing a tea trolley
- There's often little difference between first- and standard-class apart from more seating space
- Regional trains and inter-city trains usually have assigned seating (if you pick Advance fare) and you can usually pick a seat and even pick which coach (like the one with the toilet). Seats are marked with either a digital display or a paper printout.
- Almost all trains have Wi-Fi and a power outlet
- Almost every train car (or coach or carriage) has carry-on luggage racks, and most have a luggage closet that fills up quickly, so get on board quickly. Some trains have a coach set aside for larger luggage or bicycles, but not always accessible from seating areas.
- If you still have no place to put your luggage, you usually can find a jump seat at the exits, but don't block the exit
- Almost all train operators have an app you can download for free that will show you most of the information you need including estimated arrival time
- Fare types Ⓦ include *Advance*, when you book a specific train on a specific date; *Off-Peak*, which limits the trains you can travel on a specific date; *Anytime*, which lets you travel on any train that day (or within two days of the date of the ticket); *Seasonal*, which allows unlimited travel between two stations; and *Rovers and Rangers*, which allows unlimited travel within an area.

Local train service

Most larger municipalities offer train service, like the London Underground and Overground (all part of Transport for London Ⓦ). If you book through National Rail, it will include information for any local train and bus service. There are usually prepaid and smart cards for each service that offer considerable savings.

Once a train is ready to board, you can usually press a button on the outside to open the door, rather than stand there waiting for it to open like on Star Trek

Bicycle

If you're up for it, adding a bike to your narrowboat will greatly increase your range and make it easy to scout the canal ahead. Unfortunately it can be difficult to make sure your boat hire allows bicycles on board. Sometimes a brochure says yes you can take a bike on board, but then when you examine the terms and conditions, it says you can't (along with pets, barbecue grills and inflatable boats). Call, write or email your boat hire to get confirmation.

Some boat hires, however, actually rent bikes, which removes the worry. You usually have to store bikes on top of the boat, however. As usual, just do a web search for "bicycle hire" and the name of the town or canal.

Taxis

Taxis are also an option for quick trips. I had an elaborate plan for getting us from Devizes to Stonehenge, requiring several bus trips and a stop at Salisbury, but it would have meant getting up at 6 a.m. The others on the boat nixed that and we ended up asking at a pub if there was a local taxi. Our waitress obligingly called Jim the taxi driver and we were picked up the next morning at the pub at 8 a.m.

Then it was Toad's Wild Ride through narrow country lanes and Jim the taxi driver got us to Stonehenge so quickly we arrived an hour before it opened. We also enjoyed Jim's running commentary and split among four people, it was considerably cheaper than the bus fare. Again, just search for "taxi" and the name of the town and canal. In smaller towns, you'll probably find something like "Mike's Private Hire and Airport Service," rather than a large company.

Bus

Bus service remains a good option, however it can be a challenge to nail down times and pickup and drop-off locations. City, town and shire councils offer separate service.

Occasionally the planets align and you can find an organized bus tour that will take you where you want to go. The Stonehenge Tour loops through Salisbury, Old Sarum and Stonehenge, for instance. I mentioned earlier TheLoop that goes to the Falkirk Wheel. There are larger tour companies like GrayLine that can take you from several of the larger cities to whatever attraction you wish to visit. VisitBritain also has a convenient list of nationwide and local bus services.

Automobile

If you are brave enough to drive a car in the UK, you might want to view some YouTube videos about negotiating roundabouts and also at least glance at the Department of Transport's Official Highway Code booklet to familiarize yourself with the various signs and road markings. I also urge you to get a navigation system with turn-by-turn directions. Negotiating a roundabout is easier with a snooty received pronunciation voice telling you—"In 200 yards, exit left at the roundabout and take the first exit. Proceed on the A16 for two miles." And those Google maps you downloaded will help when the navigation system can't find that bed-and-breakfast in the wilds of Northumberland.

Boat hires

At the end of this chapter are links to some of the boat hires with which I'm familiar. To find more, just google the name of a waterway and add "narrowboat hire."

Organizations

Canal & River Trust
goo.gl/C86cee

The Boater's Handbook
goo.gl/K663q4

Route planning, notices, stoppages
goo.gl/JQes0U

Download a canal guide
goo.gl/FllBpv

Boater's Handbook on YouTube
youtu.be/lXn47JYXs44

Thames stream advisories
goo.gl/NIetWc

Scottish Canals
goo.gl/sK7wPa

Skipper's Guide
goo.gl/p0ngUB

Canal Works & Updates
goo.gl/Uq3wVm

Waterways Ireland
goo.gl/L3ziyT

IWAI
goo.gl/qKzkPl

IWAI maps
goo.gl/Bp5FqH

IWAI shop
goo.gl/YKXHee

IWA
goo.gl/K3OTzd

Publications

IWA *Waterways*
goo.gl/6ZiajX

Narrowboat magazine
goo.gl/dMT3bE

Towpath Talk
goo.gl/bpM2BP

Tillergraph
goo.gl/25HjqF

Waterways World
goo.gl/a7ewXt

Training

Royal Yachting Association
goo.gl/0uBlLn

Websites

Canal Junction
goo.gl/36SrVd

Narrowboat World
goo.gl/uy0Y1B

Pennine Waterways
goo.gl/cIXVC0

Narrowboat Users Group
goo.gl/JuxyK3

CanalWorld.net
goo.gl/SRvsVU

Met Office
goo.gl/HlvBa7

Youtube

Cruising the Cut
goo.gl/6HVFbA

Narrowboat Experience
goo.gl/4tAQmX

Journey with Jono
goo.gl/Qcr2aP

London Boat Girl
goo.gl/TWCcaX

CRT Channel
goo.gl/fQhMI5

Scottish Canals Channel
goo.gl/S0wzr0

List of canal trusts
goo.gl/TZuj0y

Museums

Kennet & Avon Canal Trust
goo.gl/87LyQ9

London Canal Museum
goo.gl/DMu2fl

National Waterways Museum in Cheshire
goo.gl/9ncnaM

Gloucester Waterways Museum
goo.gl/uMrBCN

Stoke Bruerne Canal Museum
goo.gl/g4N2vr

K&A Canal Trust Museum
goo.gl/ij1CWw

Etruria Industrial Museum
goo.gl/yoKmou

Books/Guides/Maps

Pearson's Companion
goo.gl/LOv12E

Collins/ Nicholson
goo.gl/0YPsxc

Our Great Canal Journeys
goo.gl/z1FWvm

Narrow Boat
goo.gl/ejFm2J

Great Waterways Journeys
goo.gl/RKRvug

My Google maps
goo.gl/ijpMNW

Ordnance Survey
goo.gl/gMjePW

How to download map
goo.gl/MpxyYZ

Google Maps iOS app
goo.gl/JZ2K0M

Google Maps Android app
goo.gl/5FNGnC

Google street view
goo.gl/xOXcLV

Open Signal.com
goo.gl/6HTLKq

Open Canal Map
goo.gl/KkiUsC

Canal PlanAC
goo.gl/xULBVi

Tourist Guides

Visit London.com
goo.gl/os49h5

Falkirk Wheel
goo.gl/1GXGuk

Visit Falkirk.com
goo.gl/V8o6sn

Visit Liverpool.com
goo.gl/mIShgy

Visit Birmingham
goo.gl/5AZkb9

Visit Britan.com
goo.gl/7NG4Z6

Visit England.com
goo.gl/X62yCq

Visit Wales.com
goo.gl/0q28C5

Visit
Scotland.com
goo.gl/Bx3Nk7

Discover
Northern Ireland
goo.gl/ASoM7g

Discover
Ireland
goo.gl/sY3bNh

Transportation

National
Rail
goo.gl/wv8LF2

Fare types
explained
goo.gl/uQD7ry

Transport
for London
goo.gl/zSOGoZ

The Stonehenge
Tour
goo.gl/W4UC4n

Grayline
Tours
goo.gl/biEhvc

Bus
services
goo.gl/jYfb7y

Roundabouts
training
youtu.be/yuqlfM-MX7g

Official Highway
Code
goo.gl/cB3oC0

Narrowboat hires

Anglo
Welsh
goo.gl/KRozBj

Black
Prince
goo.gl/MLW8Uc

Crest
Narrowboats
goo.gl/xXUqjy

Cambrian
Cruisers
goo.gl/vtCPBD

Foxhangers
goo.gl/fQBeA1

Marine
Cruises
goo.gl/z2Yl75

Pennine
Cruisers
goo.gl/NlT4aF

Conclusion

After several narrowboat trips and a solo bike trip along the canals of the Midlands, you'd think I would have had my fill of narrowboating, but something keeps drawing me back. My guess is that beyond stunning scenery, the sheer relaxation and the history of the canals, what I really cherish is how happy everybody is on the water.

Of course there's the occasional raised voice or boorish behavior, but narrowboating is a self-selecting pastime. People in a hurry, who don't appreciate nature or can't be bothered to be pleasant, generally avoid narrowboating. What you're left with then is a population of mostly polite, mostly content people who are happy to chat, remark about the weather and praise the good looks of dogs, children and boats. It would be difficult not to enjoy oneself in such company.

Another reason to go back is the fact that I always feel something was left undone on the last trip. Although I've seen any number of ducks, mallards, geese, swans, herons and egrets, I've yet to see a kingfisher, and never a vole or otter. I've yet to complete a canal ring or even cruise the entire length of a canal and we've yet to tackle one of those truly epic flight of locks, although I am perhaps alone in this desire. Each trip also gives me a chance to further appreciate the architecture, history and engineering of the canals.

I'd also like to more expertly accomplish many of the techniques I've written about. Although I've actually gotten pretty good at steering and mooring, it would be nice to casually tie a bowline without having to reference my own drawings or to avoid ramming lock gates because I mixed up forward and reverse throttle (easy to do if you face the rear of the boat). I am still essentially a beginner and forever will be compared to people who own their own boats or who live aboard a boat.

We're planning another trip in September 2018, this time on the Monmouthshire & Brecon Canal in Wales. Of course there are few locks on the canal so I can't enjoy a long flight, but I am looking forward to the many castles and the beautiful Brecon Beacons National Park, through which the canal meanders. We'll also use the trip as an opportunity to visit Bristol and especially Brunel's *SS Great Britain*.

I also hope to write another book in the *Cycling the Canals of Britain* series. I have been delayed in that desire because of a breast cancer diagnosis in October 2017. Fortunately early detection augurs a good prognosis and after a mastectomy and breast reconstruction, I should be recovered in time for our September trip.

One of the real lasting benefits of my narrowboating experience was that the memory of my trips was a very great comfort during my cancer treatment. While lying in an MRI machine, I turned the rhythmic sounds of the device into the putt-putt of a narrowboat and the harsher bleat into a horn as a boat enters or exits or tunnel. When the anesthesiologist asked where did I want to go on my drug-induced adventure just before he started my IV drip, I had a ready answer. Narrowboating is in my blood.

Glossary

999: The UK equivalent to the 911 service in the United States

aqueduct: A bridge that carries water (and in some cases narrowboats) over land and sometimes over water like the Pontcysyllte Aqueduct over the River Dee or the Dundas over the Avon

arm (of a canal): An offshoot of a canal, connecting towns or factories not on the main route of the canal

barge: What many in England call narrowboats, causing some confusion. Generally barges—like Dutch, Humber and Thames barges (also called lighters)—are wider than narrowboats.

bargee: One who works on a barge or narrowboat

beam: The long arm attached to lock gates, as in balance beam; or the width of a boat

berth: Either a bed on a boat or the space your boat occupies at a mooring

bight (of rope): A loop of rope

bitt: The small posts at the stern of the boat you tie your mooring line to, looks like a small bollard

boat hook / pole: A long pole with a point and a hook for retrieving objects that fall in the water or an even longer pole without a hook

boat lift: A device that lifts boats up or down, connecting two canals at different heights or obviating the need of many locks on a canal

boatees: People who live on narrowboats

bollard: A short post with a rounded, enlarged top to which you can tie a boat

bow: The front of the boat, usually just called the front

butty: An unpowered narrowboat that is towed

cleat: The T-shaped thing on the prow of the boat you tie your mooring line to

CRT: The Canal & River Trust, a charity that oversees 2,000 miles of canals and waterways in England and Wales

draft: The portion of the boat's hull that's underwater
Elsan: A type of chemical toilet; you're unlikely to encounter one in a hired boat
flight: A series of locks that are closely spaced
forewell / foredeck: The seating area at the front of the boat / the deck just in front of the forewell
gas locker: A storage area in the front of the boat where the liquid propane tanks and the water hose are stored
gunwale: The lip where the edge of the hull meets the top of the cabin, pronounced gunnel
gongoozler: One who enjoys watching canal activity
handcuff key: Used to unlock paddle gear at some of the more vandalism prone locks
IWA: The Inland Waterways Association is a "democratic organisation" that works with navigation authorities like the CRT
inverter: An electronic device that converts the boat's 12V electrical supply to the 240V simulating main's electricity
life ring, life preserver: The ring-shaped flotation device you throw to a drowning person
lift bridge: A bridge that must be lifted out of the way to let a boat pass
list: When the boat tilts from side to side
liveaboards: See boatees
Morse control, throttle: The maker of a popular throttle control, sometimes used to generically refer to throttle levers
nappy pins: C-shaped metal pins that hook into the piling rails along canal banks. Also called piling hooks.
narrowboat: Generally a flat-bottomed boat less than seven-feet wide
narrow/broad canal: A narrow canal has locks, bridges and tunnels only wide enough to accommodate a single narrowboat at a time, while a broad one has locks, bridges and tunnels wide enough for two narrowboats side-by-side
paddle: A sliding wooden door or panel that lets water into a lock pound
port: The left side of the boat
pound: The stretch of water between locks
pump out: Where you can get sewage pumped out of your boat
quay: A dock or wharf, pronounced "key"
saloon: The living area on a boat
sluice: An underground opening that lets water into or out of the lock pound, controlled by paddles

staircase lock: Two or more locks that share a common gate
tiller: The handle connected to the rudder that controls the course of the boat
ring route: A canal route that makes a circuit or loop
starboard: The right side of the boat
stem: The stem is the curved piece along the prow of a boat. It would be an extension of the keel, if narrowboats had keels.
stern: The rear of the boat
stern gland: The opening through which the engine's drive shaft connects to the propeller shaft. It is packed with grease, which can be renewed by the stern gland greaser.
stern styles: The different configurations of the rear of the boat: traditional (with limited room), semi-traditional (with a seating area) and cruiser (room for several people to stand within a semi-circular railing).
swing bridge: A bridge that pivots out of the way to allow a boat to pass
superstructure: The upper part of the boat (with the windows), also called the cabin top
turning a lock: The process of going through a lock. Going through a lock in one direction turns it in favor of a boat going in the other direction.
wake, wash: The wake is the turbulence left behind by the propeller and the passage of the boat through the water. Wash is the waves that reach the canal bank created by the wake.
waterways key: A Yale lock key that opens canal equipment, provided by your boat hire (or available for purchase)
water point: A fixture, almost always free, where you can get water for your boat
weed hatch: A hatch that allows access to the propeller shaft
weir: Any structure used to slow or divert a water source, either for flood control or to divert water for other purposes (such as the water source for a canal)
winding hole: A wide spot along a canal to allow a boat to turn around. Pronounced like the breezes that blow.
windlass: An L-shaped piece of metal, used as a crank, to raise/lower lock paddles or to operate lift bridges. There are usually two different-sized square holes to turn shafts for gate paddles, lift bridges and other canal gear.

Other sources

This glossary is mostly confined to terms a first-time US narrowboater might encounter. There's no need to introduce a newbie to the mysteries of uxter plates and sacrificial an-

Trine Ward's glossary
goo.gl/DfzØ6D

Jim Shead's glossary
goo.gl/uOoP6m

effingpot.com
goo.gl/oxJeSK

YouTube Anglophenia
youtube.com/user/AngopheniaTV

odes, but if you are interested in such narrowboat esoterica, there are several narrowboat glossaries online including Trines Ward's and Jim Shead's glossaries.

Of course a narrowboat glossary isn't going to help you decipher that whole "two nations divided by a common language" thing. Most people have probably watched enough British television to know that in the UK they call cookies biscuits and the hood of a car is the bonnet, but things like Cockney rhyming slang still confuses me. I've used the website effingpot.com to get through a lot of the confusion and on YouTube I've watched several of the Anglophenia episodes.

The interior of one of the stately homes we visited. This is why it's difficult to rack up the miles on a narrowboat trip—we probably spent about five hours hiking from the boat to Chirk Castle and then touring the town of Chirk.

Jennifer Petkus is a science fiction and mystery author with a particular affinity for Sherlock Holmes and Jane Austen. She's also the author of *Cycling the Canals of Britain: The Adventures of a Solitary Cyclist*. It's a travel book about her ride along the Worcester & Birmingham, Droitwich and Stratford-up-on-Avon canals.

Cycling the Canals of Britain
goo.gl/gJR67m

If you bought *Narrowboating for Beginners* at a bookstore, then thank you for supporting your local bookstore. Unfortunately your support means that you didn't automatically get the Kindle edition of the book with your purchase, but if you send me an email with a photograph of this page (with you in the picture and not obviously standing in a bookstore), then I will send you a copy of the Kindle edition.

Send an email to:
info@narrowboatingforbeginners.com
and **make the subject**:
Kindle edition with paperback purchase

The Kindle edition will be sent to you as an attachment.

I'd also love to hear about *your* narrowboat trip and any suggestions how I might improve the next edition.

Made in the USA
San Bernardino, CA
26 October 2018